THE SEARCH FOR
SIGNIFICANCE
YOUTH EDITION

THE SEARCH FOR
SIGNIFICANCE
YOUTH EDITION

Robert S. McGee
with Jack Crabtree

THOMAS NELSON
Since 1798

NASHVILLE   DALLAS   MEXICO CITY   RIO DE JANEIRO   BEIJING

Published in Nashville, Tennessee by Thomas Nelson. Thomas Nelson is a trademark of Thomas Nelson, Inc.

Thomas Nelson, Inc. titles may be purchased in bulk for educational, business, fund-raising, or sales promotional use. For information, please e-mail SpecialMarkets@ThomasNelson.com.

Material for this book is based on *The Search for Significance*, © 1998 by Robert S. McGee. Published by Thomas Nelson. All rights reserved. Text adapted for youth by Jack Crabtree, executive director of Long Island Youth for Christ.

Scripture quotations are taken from the *New Century Version*. Copyright © 1987, 1988, 1991 by W Publishing, Nashville, Tennessee. Used by permission.

Produced with the assistance of The Livingstone Corporation (www.LivingstoneCorp.com). Project staff includes Dave Veerman, Len Woods, and Mary Horner Collins.

Brand Manager: Kate Etue
Editorial Staff: Patty Crowley, Deborah Wiseman
Cover Design: Relevant Media Group
Page Design: Brecca Theele, for Book and Graphic Design, Nashville, Tennessee

Library of Congress Cataloging-in-Publication Data

McGee, Robert S.
    The search for significance / by Robert S. McGee with Jack Crabtree.—Youth ed.
    p. cm.
    ISBN 10: 0-8499-4446-5 (softcover)
    ISBN 13: 978-0-8499-4446-8 (softcover)
    1. Self-esteem—Religious aspects—Christianity. 2. Christian life. I. Crabtree, Jack, 1949–   II. Title.
BV4647.S43M387 2003
248.8'3—dc22   2003016099

Printed in the United States of America
12 QG 15 14 13 12

QG 1D-26-12

CONTENTS

INTRODUCTION

Look around you. Have you ever wondered what shaped the lives of those you know? Sometimes you might think it must be how smart they are or how much education they have obtained. You might even think people are the way they are because, well, they really didn't have any other choice. But the fact of the matter is that we are the way we are because of the way we think about ourselves. And because of Christ we've been given the chance to think about ourselves as the new identity He made us when we accepted Him.

You have a great opportunity to discover truths that will protect you from having your life determined by fear—the fear of rejection, the fear of failure, the fear of punishment and shame. Those of us who have lived a little longer than you look back and realize that our experience of life could have been so much greater if we had known these truths.

Another powerful truth you'll learn in these pages is just how much God really loves you. Your awareness of this love will give you strength to deal with whatever life throws at you. Another bonus is that it will protect you from getting into destructive relationships. Most importantly, you'll discover that God has a role for you, an exciting part for you to play in what He's doing in the world. There is a tendency today to believe that young people cannot make a difference or be expected to have a real commitment to Christ. I don't believe that this is true. The main problem that most young Christians have is the same one older adult Christians have—they don't know who they are or what they are supposed to be about. Unfortunately, they are taught little, and even less is expected from them. This is not God's view of you at all.

As you read this book, listen for God to point out to you what He wants you to know. Don't read it to just gain facts. Facts will do you little good. You have an incredible opportunity to learn truths that will make a difference not only now but for the rest of your life. Hundreds of thousands of people have already made these discoveries. Now it's your turn.

1

SOMETHING'S MISSING

Teenagers have a pretty simple job description—just two major assignments to accomplish and eight years to get them done:

1

Get along and fit in with your peers.

2

Develop your own identity.

The SAT scores, the sports teams, and all the schoolwork are overrated as "critical steps to becoming a teenage success" compared to the lessons you learn in those years between leaving childhood and entering adulthood. The job is simple—*find out who you are and how you fit into this messed-up world.*

Whoever thought such a simple job could get you into so much trouble? Life was easier when Mom and Dad were calling all the shots. Unless you were a child prodigy at getting your own way, your parents' agenda was your agenda. No questions asked.

But it wasn't a total waste of time. You learned a lot about life by watching them. What you saw and heard became the foundation of what you think about life and who you are as a person today. So before you even signed on to be a teenager, the wet cement in your brain was already starting to dry. You had a pretty good idea about who you were and how life worked by the time you reached double digits. It wasn't all good, but life sure seemed more peaceful and secure as a kid than it did once puberty started changing your body and rocking your world.

Somehow when those growth hormones started streaking through your body, your world began to change. There was no going back. And you will never be the same. It can be a jack-hammer time of life—busting up all your assumptions about what is right or wrong, true or false. Your identity is no longer built around your parents. In fact, the thought of growing up to be like them is now one of your biggest fears. You fight for your freedom and blow holes in the protective bubble your parents carefully constructed around you. There is a fresh, unexplored world out there. You want to be part of it.

What your parents don't fill you in on about life you learn from television, movies, and music. If you're like most teens, the amount of time you spend watching and listening to the lessons of love and sex, being cool and looking hot, developing power and attaining success amounts to more than double the time you spend in school. With eyes focused on the screen and ears encased in headphones, the basic expectations of happiness, fulfillment, and the rules of life are embedded into the creases of your brain and deep into your soul.

So, how is it for you so far?

Is life all it's cracked up to be?

Or is something missing?

WHY AM I SO UNHAPPY?

Mark's senior year is wearing him down. Life has been tense at home. He is waitlisted at the colleges where he applied. So basically he's worked really hard, and some committee decides he is second choice at best. "Second choice" sums up exactly how Mark feels about life. If he doesn't get in, he will never hear the end of it from his dad. You try hard to do the best you can, but your parents and teachers can always find something wrong with you. What you do is never good enough.

Mark's dad is still talking about the bad grades he got his freshman year. He won't let it go. He knew then that Mark would never get into college. These days Mark stays out of the house and hangs with friends. Even with friends, Mark has the feeling that when they leave for college (and he inevitably stays home), they won't stay in touch. All those guys will make new friends. That's a great feeling—they're only your friends until someone better comes along. Second choice again. Isn't life great?

At sixteen, Amanda isn't doing so great. Her mom caught her cutting herself in the bathroom and took her to a therapist for teenage girls. Amanda hates being there—she feels like she's some kind of psycho-case. She's unhappy and depressed about life, like most of her friends at school. What's weird about that?

Her father left years ago. She fights with her mom about her friends, going out, and the clothes she wears. Her mom calls Amanda a sponge because, in her opinion, she just soaks up the attitude and behavior of everybody she's around. That is track #3 on her mom's *I'm Really Worried About You* greatest hits and lectures CD. She can repeat it back to her mom word for word. As the therapist probes about feelings and missing her father, Amanda puts up the hard shell. Life stinks. Who can change that?

Nobody will ever love me.

If people really knew me, they wouldn't like me.

I've been a failure all my life.

I guess I'll always be a failure.

I'll never be able to change.

Not even God really cares about me.

SOMETHING *IS* MISSING

People say the years between twelve and twenty are the best years of your life. If these are the best years, then life is a cruel joke. But lots of us have some serious reactions. The young girls starving themselves to be thin are not a joke. The anger boiling over in many young men has school counselors and parents in a major panic. A spirit of depression and hopelessness presses down on young people who don't like themselves or feel like they have no significant place or role in this world.

Some people call it self-esteem. Others say self-worth. Whatever it is—it is the feeling of significance deep inside us that is crucial to our emotional, spiritual, and social stability. Everyone wants to be happy and successful, and to regard himself or herself as a worthwhile human being. What's so bad about that?

The problem is that more and more teenagers are asking, "Is this all there is to life?" They are not happy about being young and living in this world. They don't like

Think About This. Jesus Christ told His disciples: "You will know the truth, and the truth will make you free" (John 8:32). The purpose of this book is to identify the truth that Jesus said would set us free, and then apply it to our lives.

being who they are. *Happy. Successful. Believe in yourself.* It's just hype for a lot of youth today.

Before everyone starts shaking their heads, let's ask ourselves: "Could it be that what we have been told about fulfillment is a lie? That chasing after personal success, status, beauty, wealth, and the approval of others is a dead-end street? Is it possible that we have been told the biggest, boldest lies about what is most important in life?"

DOES GOD CARE?

The Bible tells us that God created us each individually, and He constantly keeps His eye on us. Do we know we are significant and valuable to God? Jesus said that God knows details like the number of hairs on our head, sees everything we do, and loves us personally and unconditionally. Jesus said that God is not some distant, uninvolved deity but, in fact, wants to know us authentically and have a moment-by-moment relationship with us. Even more remarkable to our modern minds is the fact that this personal God loves us and wants to know when we are mad at Him, messed up by the mistakes of life, or even when we simply don't care anymore. God offers unconditional love and acceptance as the basis for a strong sense of personal self-worth. Can you believe that?

GOD'S ORIGINAL DESIGN

The way you see life right now isn't the way it started. When God created the first people, Adam and Eve, He made them to live in intimate fellowship with Him. Adam and Eve were remarkable, magnificent people made in God's image. They were placed in a perfect environment where all their physical needs were met. They were responsible to oversee paradise with all its vegetation and animals. They knew God and walked and talked with Him. Adam and Eve were perfect in body, mind, and spirit.

WHAT WENT WRONG?

Adam and Eve had a visitor in the Garden of Eden who came to destroy what God had given to them. Lucifer (the name means "Morning Star") had been an angel of the highest rank created to glorify God. He was clothed in beauty and power as he served in the presence of God. Sadly, Lucifer's pride caused him to rebel against God. When this happened, he and one-third of all the angels were expelled from heaven.

It was the same Lucifer who came to visit Adam and Eve in the form of a serpent. If he could get Adam and Eve to rebel against God, they would lose their authority and their perfection.

They would become slaves to Satan and sin[1] and be under God's wrath and judgment.[2] If this worked, Satan would screw up Adam and Eve's relationship with God and destroy God's great plan for these people He had created.

Jesus called Satan "the father of lies." Satan deceived Eve by getting her to doubt God's honesty and suggesting that she would gain greater power and wisdom apart from God. When she ate the forbidden fruit, she traded God's truth for Satan's lie, believing it would make her become like God. When she offered the same opportunity to Adam, he accepted and turned away from the love and security he had known with God. It was a sad day that changed the future of the world, and the future of all who have been born in the years to follow.

WHAT DOES THIS HAVE TO DO WITH ME?

When Adam and Eve did this, they lost their secure status with God and began to struggle with feelings of arrogance, inadequacy, and despair, valuing the opinions of others more than the opinions of God. This robbed Adam of his true self-worth and put him on the continual but fruitless quest for significance through personal success and the approval of others.

As descendants of Adam and Eve, we are born with a sinful nature that rebels against God and attempts to find security and purpose in this world apart from Him. We stand guilty before

God and deserve His wrath. Nothing we can do as human beings can pay the penalty for our sins against God.

What are those sins? We could make a long list of specific attitudes and actions. The best overall explanation of sin is that we ignore God (the real God) and act like we are god (not the real god), doing whatever we think is best for us. In the process, we disobey many of the specific commands God has given us. Worst of all, we go through most days without acknowledging that the God who created us is a very real part of our lives. We ignore Him and try our best to take care of life in our own human strength.

The results are predictable. Amanda and Mark and millions of other people have found out how empty life is without God.

In what ways have you turned away from God, and how often?

What experiences have made you feel that life without God was empty?

WHY THEY CALL IT "GOOD NEWS"

Just when our situation was hopeless, God acted on our behalf to pay the penalty for all these sins that we have committed by sending His own Son, Jesus Christ, into our world. It was God's plan that Jesus would willingly die on the cross taking the punishment, as if He had committed our sins. This sacrifice made us pure, and nothing demonstrates God's love for us more clearly than His giving Jesus to die for us. Through Christ's death on the cross our relationship with God has been restored. We can experience His nature and character in our life as we live in a spiritual relationship with Him and show His love to the entire world.

Through Jesus Christ we experience the security and significance for which we were created—not just in eternity beyond the death of our human bodies, but here on earth as well. Adam and Eve's sin had tragic consequences on our world and on each one of us, but through God's plan of redemption we can be brought back to God and start our relationship with Him all over again.

God has made it possible for every person to be restored to Him. Jesus clearly explained God's wonderful plan when He told Nicodemus:

God loved the world so much that he gave his one and only Son so that whoever believes in him may not be lost, but have eternal life. God did not send his Son into the world to judge the world guilty, but to save the world through him.[3]

Getting reconnected to God is not about how you can pay God back for the sins you've committed—you can't. And it's not about what you can do for God or about being a nice person or about giving your money away. That's not ever enough. We can't make ourselves right in God's sight; only our belief and trust in Christ's death and resurrection are sufficient to pay for our sin and separation from God.

Paul wrote about this gift from God:

I mean that you have been saved by grace through believing. You did not save yourselves; it was a gift from God. It was not the result of your own efforts, so you cannot brag about it.[4]

Then he explained to Titus what God did for us:

But when the kindness and love of God our Savior was shown, he saved us because of his mercy. It was not because of good deeds we did to be right with him. He saved us through the washing that made us new people through the Holy Spirit.[5]

If you want to receive God's unconditional love, you can respond by trusting in Christ and accepting His payment for your sins. You can say the words of this prayer to express your faith:

Lord Jesus, I need You. I want You to be my Savior and the Lord of my life. I accept Your death on the cross as the complete payment for my sins. Thank You for forgiving me and for giving me new life. Help me understand Your love and power, so that my life will bring honor to You. Amen.

CAN GOD CHANGE YOUR LIFE?

When you trust Christ, you experience many wonderful changes.

⇒ All your sins are forgiven: past, present, and future.[6]

⇒ You become a child of God.[7]

⇒ You receive eternal life.[8]

⇒ You are delivered from Satan's domain and transferred into the kingdom of Christ.[9]

⇒ Christ comes to dwell within you.[10]

⇒ You become a new creation.[11]

⇒ God declares you righteous.[12]

⇒ You enter into a love relationship with God.[13]

⇒ God completely accepts you.[14]

THE CHOICE IS YOURS

You would think that everyone hearing this good news would run to God and put their faith and trust in what Jesus Christ has done for them. Sadly that is not so. We are extremely stubborn and really quite full of pride. Rather than receive God's unconditional love, we create false gods in our own image when we should be humbling ourselves before the real, living God. This is how Paul describes it:

> They knew God, but they did not give glory to God or thank him. Their thinking became useless. Their foolish minds were filled with darkness. They said they were wise, but they became fools. They traded the glory of God who lives forever for the worship of idols made to look like earthly people, birds, animals, and snakes.[15]

God has given us plenty of physical and spiritual evidence to know that He is real:

> But since the beginning of the world those things have been easy to understand by what God has made. So people have no excuse for the bad things they do.[16]

We ignore the evidence and only believe what we can understand with our human minds. We make substitute gods to worship and look to them for comfort rather than the real God:

Because they did these things, God left them and let them go their sinful way, wanting only to do evil. As a result, they became full of sexual sin, using their bodies wrongly with each other. They traded the truth of God for a lie. They worshiped and served what had been created instead of the God who created those things, who should be praised forever. Amen.[17]

God lets us follow the temporary pleasures (money, sex, and power) in our search for who we are. All our human answers disappoint us because we exchange the truth for a lie and reduce God to something that we try to humanly understand and explain.

Satan's lie still thrives. Many schools teach humanism, the godless philosophy that humans are intended to heighten the dignity of man. But when you remove God as Creator, then humans are merely the product of evolutionary chance and no different than animals or the physical world.

It's your choice—you can either go to God to find out the truth about who you are and what the purpose of your life is, or you can let other people make the rules about what success is and who is valuable.

WHY READ THIS BOOK?

This book explores the four major deceptions Satan tries to sell us about who we are. Even those of us who have put our trust in Christ often find ourselves believing these deceptions. You can learn to counter those lies with God's plan to bring us back to the destiny for which He originally created us—to become like Jesus Christ.

Satan, of course, is absolutely opposed to our becoming like Christ. He has convinced most of the world that this equation of life is true:

$$Self\text{-}Worth = Performance + Others' \; Opinions$$

If we base our worth on our ability to perform or on the ever-changing approval of others, we should not be surprised when we are tormented by thoughts of insecurity, fear, and anger. The real choice is whether our true value is based on our behavior and the approval of others or on what God says is true about us.

Our choice is important because our behavior is often a reflection of our beliefs about who we are—consistent with what we think to be true about ourselves.[18] We have compelling, God-given needs for love, acceptance, and purpose. Most of us will go to virtually any length to meet those needs. The power of Satan's lie is strong when we are feeling weak. The challenge and the choice remain: Can you trust God's complete acceptance of you as His son or daughter and allow Him to free you from your dependency on success and the approval of others?

//

PERSONAL INVENTORY

Answer these questions and discuss them with a friend.

1 When do you feel really far away from God?

2 When do you feel really close to God?

3 Where are you right now with God?

4 Have you prayed and invited Jesus to come into your life?

5 If so, what changes have you seen God make in you since receiving Christ?

6 If not, what are your reasons for not responding to what God has done for you?

7 On what do you base your self-worth? or What makes you feel good about being *you*?

///

VERSES TO READ:

1. Romans 6:17
2. Ephesians 2:3
3. John 3:16–17
4. Ephesians 2:8–9
5. Titus 3:4–5
6. Colossians 2:13–14
7. John 1:12; Romans 8:15
8. John 5:24
9. Colossians 1:13
10. Colossians 1:27; Revelation 3:20
11. 2 Corinthians 5:17

12. 2 Corinthians 5:21
13. 1 John 4:9–11
14. Colossians 1:19–22
15. Romans 1:21–23
16. Romans 1:20
17. Romans 1:24–25
18. Proverbs 23:6–7

2

THE PERFORMANCE TRAP

"I MUST NOT FAIL"

Alexis has never made a B in her life. Every report card is the same—straight As . . . 4.0 GPA . . . pure academic perfection. But lately her chemistry class has been really hard. Alexis is ticked off at her "irresponsible jock" lab partner for the "pathetic" 71 they got on a major project a few weeks back. Thanks to that one low grade, she basically has to ace tomorrow's final exam to pull an A for the semester. Truth is, she's not ready for this test, and what's worse, she's not sure she can get ready in time. Could all this explain why she is in the bathroom sobbing and throwing up at 11:45 P.M.?

Justin hates to lose. Everybody is over at Brandon's playing Bond on his family's giant plasma-screen TV. Brandon says, "Hey, Justin. Grab the controller. I want *you!*" Justin smiles, shakes his head, and says, "Sorry, man. Another time. I'm late. Gotta head out." Does

Justin really have to rush home, or is his unwillingness to play against Brandon perhaps tied to the fact that he knows Brandon would crush him in the game?

Are you more likely to tolerate failure in your friends' lives or your own?

How much does the fear of embarrassment keep you from taking on new challenges?

What are some specific things that might be different about your life if you could get beyond the fear of failure?

So far in our search for real significance, we've seen that Christians have a sworn enemy called Satan. The devil is real, and he's *not* someone we should dismiss lightly. Satan hates the people of God with a fierce passion. Jesus called him a murderer.[1] The apostle Peter compared him to a vicious lion, hungry for a kill.[2] His only goal now is to try to ruin our lives . . . by any and every means possible. He's a ruthless accuser,[3] and a world–class tempter. Spewing out one lie after another,[4] he blinds people from seeing and understanding God's truth,[5] the truth that will set them free.[6]

The same subtle strategies and deceitful schemes he used on Adam and Eve are unleashed on us. Relentlessly, Satan zeros in on our beliefs—all those conscious and subconscious ideas we base our lives on. Why does he focus there? Because he knows that we act on what we truly think and believe. Beliefs determine behavior. If the devil can get us to believe the wrong things—

about God and ourselves—then he knows it'll be a piece of cake for him to get us to act in wrong ways.

In a fallen world, full of rebellious people and dominated by Satan, it's tough, even for Christians, to think correctly. Just because we've pledged allegiance to Christ doesn't mean we automatically believe all the right things. The fact is, we'll have to spend the rest of our earthly lives identifying Satan's lies in our lives, renouncing them and replacing them with God's truth. It's only as we work at renewing our minds (learning to think like Jesus)[7] that we are able to live radically different lives.

The apostle Paul put it this way in his letter to the Christians in Ephesus:

> In the Lord's name, I tell you this. Do not continue living like those who do not believe. Their thoughts are worth nothing. They do not understand, and they know nothing, because they refuse to listen. So they cannot have the life that God gives. They have lost all feeling of shame, and they use their lives for doing evil. They continually want to do all kinds of evil.
>
> But what you learned in Christ was not like this. I know that you heard about him, and you are in him, so you were taught the truth that is in Jesus. You were taught to leave your old self—to stop living the evil way you lived before. That old self becomes worse, because people are fooled by the evil things they want to do. But you were taught to be made new in your hearts, to become a new person. That new person is made to be like God—made to be truly good and holy.[8]

Think About This. "Be sure that no one leads you away with false and empty teaching that is only human, which comes from the ruling spirits of this world, and not from Christ."⁹

To be led away by false teaching (or "cheated by empty philosophy and high-sounding nonsense," as the Living Bible words it) means we have become prisoners of dangerously wrong beliefs. It means we have bought into some of Satan's false promises that will never come true.

Notice the two options: either darkened understanding and knowing nothing *or* being made new in your heart and mind—a spiritual renewal of your thoughts and attitudes.

That's what this book is really all about—changing the way we live by changing the way we think. It's about recognizing Satan's lies, getting rid of them, and choosing instead to believe "the truth that is in Jesus."¹⁰

In this chapter we want to focus on one of Satan's most successful strategies and one of his most destructive schemes. It's a sick idea that entraps millions of people (including lots of Christians), robbing them of joy. Call it the "Performance Trap."

WHAT IS THE PERFORMANCE TRAP?

The Performance Trap is the false promise that success will bring us ultimate fulfillment and happiness. Those who buy into this lie build their lives and base their actions on this destructive belief:

I have to accomplish certain things in order to feel good about myself.

Or we could state that same belief in these terms:

If I fail to reach certain goals, then I will feel like a total loser.

If you look around, you can see countless ways your friends and classmates fall victim to the Performance Trap. Here are just a few: I'll feel good about myself if . . .

⇒ I make the cheerleading squad.

⇒ I earn a spot on the football team.

⇒ I make Eagle Scout.

⇒ I make honor roll.

⇒ I get a part in the school play.

⇒ I get a *speaking* part in the play.

⇒ I make a really high score on my SAT/ACT.

⇒ I get a scholarship to a certain college.

⇒ I lose five pounds.

⇒ I'm able to bench-press 250 pounds.

⇒ I win first place at the science fair.

⇒ I get hired for my ideal summer job.

Most honest teenagers can relate to at least a few of those thoughts and feelings. Perhaps deep inside you feel an almost overwhelming need to achieve. Maybe your self-image is totally wrapped up in how well you perform. Maybe you are driven by a powerful fear of failure.

The problem with needing to succeed in order to feel good about ourselves is that no one can do it all the time. Sometimes we have an off day. Sometimes another person outperforms us. Some failure is inevitable—even for the truly great.

What are some other examples of the Performance Trap?

⇒

⇒

⇒

There was once a Gatorade advert with basketball legend Michael Jordan. He said:

I have missed more than 9,000 shots in my career. I have lost almost 300 games. On 26 occasions I have been entrusted to take the game-winning shot . . . and missed. I have failed over and over and over again in my life. And that is why . . . I succeed.

Failure isn't fun, but it is a fact of life. Nobody gets it right every single time (not even the greatest in their fields!). Did you know, for example, that Babe Ruth had almost twice as many strikeouts as home runs? The point is this: Basing your self-worth on how perfectly you perform is setting yourself up for continual frustration. It guarantees that you will spend most of your time living in fear of failure, and the rest of your time feeling like a loser.

Is that what you want out of life? Does that sound like a good way to spend your time?

"Success is never final. Failure is never fatal. It's courage that counts."
—Winston Churchill, Prime Minister of England

Do you feel you have to be successful in order to feel good about yourself?

What things do you believe you need to succeed in to feel good about yourself?

//

IS THE PERFORMANCE TRAP TRIPPING YOU UP?

Being caught in the Performance Trap creates a tremendous fear of failure. And if we don't deal with it, this fear can lead to some seriously wrong attitudes . . . and some very unhealthy actions. The following list of "symptoms" describes a number of wrong beliefs and behaviors that commonly occur when we are ruled by a fear of failure (or an obsession with success). Obviously, some of these symptoms can be caused by other factors. However, if you "look in the mirror," so to speak, and recognize one or more of these characteristics in your own life, you will be taking the first important step in escaping from the Performance Trap.

//

SYMPTOMS

Perfectionism
This is one of the most common symptoms of the fear of failure. A perfectionist is a person who freaks out over any kind of mistake or failure—even little ones. Instead of focusing on the ninety-nine test questions he got right and feeling a sense of accomplishment, the perfectionist will obsess over the one question he missed and beat himself up for it. Perfectionists are extremely motivated—

sometimes *driven*—in their quest to achieve. However, their motivation really stems from a fear of failure. The belief that drives them? "I *can't* fail. I *have* to succeed, or I will no longer feel good about myself."

Avoidance of Risks

This is another clue that a person has been captured by the fear of failure. This is the point guard who resists taking a shot even when she's wide open. Her reasoning? "If I don't shoot, I won't ever miss." Risk-avoiders are unwilling to do anything they might not succeed at. Sometimes they miss out on fun, new activities, and even potential friendships because the risk of failure seems too great.

Anger and Resentment

These symptoms occur when we think our performance is being criticized. The idea here is that any bit of criticism (even well-intended advice) suggests that we have failed in some way, and that feeling of failure brings about a loss of self-esteem. An example of this might be the student who strongly resents a tough teacher. The teacher demands excellence and goes wild with her red pen when correcting essays. Why? Because she's mad at the world? No, because she wants her students to do their absolute best. She is trying to prepare them for the rigors of college. Meanwhile, the bitter student regards the teacher's corrections and point deductions simply as a personal attack. Lower grades rob him of good feelings about himself, and so he lashes out, "She's such a jerk!"

Pride

When a person caught in the Performance Trap achieves success, he may become cocky and arrogant and subtly look down on all the "failures," known as friends, around him. Pride sometimes disguises itself as self-confidence, but that's all it is—a disguise. It's a mask we wear to hide our fear of failure. What's more, the prideful feelings we experience as a result of success come and go, because failure is a sobering fact of life.

Anxiety and Fear

The stressed-out, "doom-and-gloom" feeling that weighs us down when we think something in our lives is about to go wrong is called *anxiety*. It's what you feel when you prepare to retake your SAT for the fourth time. So much hinges on how well you do, and you're certain you'll screw up. *What if I don't raise my score? What if I can't get into Princeton? What if . . . what if?* This fretfulness, a first cousin to fear, usually occurs whenever we are put in situations where we sense the strong possibility of failure. The greater the risk of failure, the more anxiety and fear grip our hearts and control our decisions. You call *this* living?

Depression

This is one of the most crippling symptoms of the Performance Trap. Failure—especially repeated failure—prompts us to conclude that we are worthless. "I can't do anything right." "I'm such a loser." "Everybody else is better than me at everything." When we begin to believe such lies, and depression sets in, we will react in one of two ways. Some people become lethargic and passive, believing there is no hope for change or success. Others become angry at the world, striking out at everything and everyone.

Dishonesty

Maybe you know some friends who are so scared of even the *thought* of failure that they will do almost anything to avoid it. Think, for example, of the athlete who uses steroids, or the honor student who plagiarizes his term paper. The fear of failure prompts many to deny the truth and blatantly lie in a desperate attempt to succeed. And, on the flip side, think of how many people exaggerate the truth in order to take credit for certain accomplishments. Consider how tempting it sometimes is to "spin" certain situations so that we come off looking good and others end up taking the blame. People who are desperate to succeed will resort to desperate measures.

Chemical Addiction

Many people attempt to ease the sting of failure by using drugs and/or alcohol. People who use are sending a surefire signal that they do not feel good about themselves. They view that false high as a way to escape, at least for a short time, the intense pain of not "measuring up." Getting loaded or getting high is a bit pleasurable at first, and it relieves (temporarily) the pressure to perform. However, as we all learn in Physics 101, whatever goes up must come down. Once the trip or binge is over, a person crashes back into reality. It's then that many users fall into deeper despair and become convinced they'll *never* be able to cope with real life.

If you see any of these eight symptoms at work in your life, then you are, at some level, a victim of the Performance Trap. And if you wrestle deeply with a fear of failure, then you can't possibly feel very good about yourself or be very excited about life. Would you like to discover just how deep your fear of failure goes?

POP QUIZ

Remember, our fear of failure comes from the false belief that says, *I have to accomplish certain things in order to feel good about myself.* How affected are *you* by this belief? One way to find out is to take this quiz.

Now I know what some of you are thinking: A test! Omigosh! What if I miss one? What if I fail? Relax. This isn't that kind of test. In fact, it's actually more of a personal inventory. It's for *your* eyes only. This is just a simple tool designed for you to get a more accurate sense of how deeply you've been affected by wrong ideas about success and failure. You can't address a problem until you first know how severe it is, right? So . . . are you ready to dive in?

Each of the following statements has seven possible answers. Read each statement and then write the appropriate number in the blank space next to each statement.

1 = Always
2 = Very Often

3 = Often

4 = Sometimes

5 = Seldom

6 = Very Seldom

7 = Never

_____ 1. Because of the fear that I won't do well, I often avoid joining in certain activities.

_____ 2. When I sense I might fail in some important area, I become seriously nervous and anxious.

_____ 3. I get really stressed.

_____ 4. I feel anxious for no real reason.

_____ 5. I am a perfectionist.

_____ 6. I have to defend my mistakes.

_____ 7. There are certain areas in which I have to succeed.

_____ 8. I get depressed when I fail.

_____ 9. I get mad at people who do things that make me look like I don't know what I'm doing or like I'm stupid.

_____ 10. I am critical of myself.

_____ **TOTAL** (Add up the numbers in the ten blanks.)

Interpreting the Results

If your score was:

57–70: Congratulations! You are virtually free from the fear of failure. (Maybe you should be writing this chapter!)

47–56: Good! You have a very small fear of failure. It may be only certain situations that cause you trouble.

37–46: You have a moderate to strong fear of failure. It is likely that a good number of your decisions are designed to minimize your chance of failing.

27–36: You have a high fear of failure. Your emotional lows will almost always be a result of your fear of failure or the belief that you have already failed in some way. Nearly all of your decisions are designed to keep you as far from failing as possible.

0–26: You have an overwhelming fear of failure. Experiences of failure fill your memories. You are likely depressed.

If you ended up with a score that is lower than you'd prefer, don't panic. This isn't the final word on your life. It's just a snapshot of where you happen to be right now. Nearly everyone has struggled (or does struggle) with the fear of failure to some degree. But God doesn't want us to remain hurting and confused victims of the Performance Trap. The rest of this chapter will guide you through God's awesome solution for freeing people from the fear of failure.

GOD'S SOLUTION TO THE PERFORMANCE TRAP

God's solution to the Performance Trap is for us to understand what Jesus Christ has done for us and in us. God knows that because of our frequent failures, we can never perform well enough to please ourselves, much less live up to His perfect standards. The harder we try not to fail, the more we seem to mess up, and the more discouraged we become. But God, because of His great love, has worked through Christ to help us solve once and for all our performance problem. Let's look at what the Bible says:

> Since we have been made right with God by our faith, we have peace with God. This happened through our Lord Jesus Christ.[11]

> After Adam sinned once, he was judged guilty. But the gift of God is different. God's free gift came after many sins, and it makes people right with God. . . . So as one sin of Adam brought the punishment of death to all people, one good act that Christ did makes all people right with God. And that brings true life for all.[12]

Go back and linger over some of those amazing phrases! *Peace with God . . . free gift . . . all people right with God.* That last phrase sums up what these verses are saying about what Christ has done for us.

This is all about what Christ did for us—dying on the cross to pay the penalty for our sins against God. And as Romans 5:1 indicates, we experience it "by our faith." That means when we trust in Christ's sacrifice, when we put our faith in Him rather than our own abilities to succeed, we are completely forgiven. All our failures (past, present, and future) are dealt with by Christ's forgiveness and love. We no longer have to fear failure (or anything else!).

Another verse in the Bible describes justification even further:

> Christ had no sin, but God made him become sin so that in
> Christ we could become right with God.[13]

What does this mean? Basically that God performed a miraculous exchange. He took our sins and failures, our rebellious acts and screwups, and poured all of it on Christ as He hung there on the cross. Jesus was literally the scapegoat for the human race. He acted as our substitute, taking the terrible shame and punishment we deserved. Somehow, during His horrifying crucifixion, Jesus became the very essence of sin.

But that's not all. When Jesus rose from His horrible death, He was perfect, clean, and totally pleasing to God the Father once again. The Bible word for this is *righteousness*, which really just means "rightness." Christ has an infinite, unending supply of righteousness with which to cover us. And when we put our faith in Him that's exactly what He does! In the same way that God took our imperfection and poured it on the crucified Christ, He then took the resurrected Christ's perfection and poured it on believers!

The implications of God's "justification" are stunning, mind-boggling, breathtaking. And they are essential to escaping from the Performance Trap. When you put your trust in Jesus, when you called upon Him to deliver you, then:

⇒ Christ's horrible death paid for *all* your sins. Every single one of your failures, rebellious acts, terrible performances, and mistakes was forgiven and forgotten. In that instance, God declared you "not guilty."

⇒ Christ's perfect righteousness flooded your life. You received full credit for His perfect life. You were declared "acceptable and pleasing to God." And that's exactly the way He sees you.

In other words, the pressure is off. To the One who really matters most—God—you completely measure up. You are already *totally* accepted. His approval is yours, forever, no matter what you do or don't do. Because of Christ, God will always be completely pleased with who you are—even when you fail.

If all that is hard for you to swallow, then hear it straight from God's mouth:

> At one time you were separated from God. You were his enemies in your minds, and the evil things you did were against God. But now God has made you his friends again. He did this through Christ's death in the body so that he might bring you into God's presence as people who are holy, with no wrong, and with nothing of which God can judge you guilty.[14]

Do you see it? If you became the most successful person in human history, you could not increase your worth to God. And if you failed miserably for the rest of your life, you could not decrease your worth to God. He has completely forgiven you for all your sins—the ones already committed and the ones you haven't even thought of yet. When God looks at you, He sees the righteousness of Christ and He smiles with approval. That "right-ness" is the most precious item in the entire universe, and guess what? It belongs to you!

This is why you do not have to be paralyzed by the fear of failure. You can be free of its symptoms that bring you down. Since the Bible is true, God is as fully pleased with you as He is with His Son, Jesus Christ.

Think About This. "Make the Lord and His immense love for you the basis of your personal worth. Define yourself radically as one beloved by God. . . . Accept that, and let it become the most important thing in your life." —John Eagan, a Milwaukee schoolteacher

One final note: Because God has completely justified you, you may be wondering, *If I'm fully accepted by God and nothing I do can alter His love for me, why not go ahead and do whatever I want, even sin?* Here are four good reasons not to embrace such a lifestyle:

1 God hates sin, and it breaks His heart when His children defiantly disobey.

2 Sin is destructive, and always, *always* has consequences that bring pain and heartache into our lives, as well as the lives of those around us.[15]

3 God will not punish Christians in eternity (Jesus has taken that divine judgment for us), but because He loves us too much to let us mess up our lives, He will discipline us in the present.[16]

4 Christ wants us to be so in love with Him that our devotion and passion for Him keep us faithful.[17]

RECAP

To some degree, just about everyone is affected by the Performance Trap. Deep inside, we have bought the satanic lie that "in order to feel good about ourselves, we have to meet certain standards or accomplish certain goals." We've all experienced the crushing frustration of failure firsthand, and we have created elaborate strategies to avoid feeling its sting. The result is an oppressive lifestyle of fear, shame, and stress, rather than the peace and confidence and joy that Jesus promises.

However, God has made it possible for Christians to escape

this painful and often dangerous Performance Trap through what the Bible calls *justification*. Justification means that God, in His love, has completely forgiven our sins and totally has covered us with the perfection of Christ. The result is that, despite our continuing failures, we are fully pleasing to God.

"So now, those who are in Christ Jesus are not judged guilty. Through Christ Jesus the law of the Spirit that brings life made me free from the law that brings sin and death.[18]"

So go ahead and do your best in school or sports or whatever activity you're involved in, but realize this: Even if you mess up, you're still safe and secure in God's love and acceptance. He doesn't think any less of you, and neither should you.

THE "RENEWING MY MIND" PROJECT

Since our beliefs determine how we think about God and ourselves, and since they govern the lifestyle choices we make, it's important for us to spend time "reprogramming" the way we think. We need to reject the devil's lies and the world's bogus ideas and replace them with God's truth. The Bible refers to this lifelong process as "renewing our minds."[19]

As we've seen in this chapter, God wants us to abandon the foolish and frustrating notion that we have to accomplish certain things in order to feel good about ourselves.

The following four Bible passages teach some of the correct

beliefs that can help you escape the Performance Trap. It would be good to spend some time memorizing these verses. It would be even better to follow that up by meditating on these truths. By meditation, we don't mean the mindless, mystical, mumbo jumbo practiced by some. On the contrary, biblical meditation involves actively rolling the truths of God's Word around in our minds and thinking deeply about what they mean and what difference they make. Think of meditation as "marinating your mind" in God's truth. You basically let God's Word soak into your soul, imparting its flavor and essence to all that you are and do.

> But when the kindness and love of God our Savior were shown, he saved us because of his mercy. It was not because of good deeds we did to be right with him. He saved us through the washing that made us new people through the Holy Spirit.[20]

CORRECT BELIEF #1

I thank God that my actions (successes or failures) have *nothing* to do with Christ's love for me.

> Since we have been made right with God by our faith, we have peace with God. This happened through our Lord Jesus Christ.[21]

CORRECT BELIEF #2

I thank God that since He has taken away my sin and given me Christ's righteousness, I am now right with God.

> Christ had no sin, but God made him become sin so that in Christ we could become right with God.[22]

CORRECT BELIEF #3

I thank God that I am now as pure and righteous and pleasing to Him as His Son, Jesus Christ!

> At one time you were separated from God. You were his enemies in your minds, and the evil things you did were against God. But now God has made you his friends again.[23]

CORRECT BELIEF #4

I thank God that I don't have to dwell on my past sins or present-day failures—He has forgotten them and so should I!

> Their sins and the evil things they do—I will not remember.[23]

VERSES TO READ:

1. John 8:44
2. 1 Peter 5:8
3. Revelation 12:10
4. John 8:44
5. 2 Corinthians 4:4
6. John 8:32
7. Romans 12:2
8. Ephesians 4:17–24
9. Colossians 2:8
10. Ephesians 4:21
11. Romans 5:1
12. Romans 5:16, 18
13. 2 Corinthians 5:21–22
14. Colossians 1:21–22
15. Galatians 6:7
16. Hebrews 12:5–6
17. 2 Corinthians 5:14
18. Romans 8:1–2
19. Romans 12:2; Ephesians 4:23
20. Titus 3:4–5
21. Romans 5:1
22. 2 Corinthians 5:21
23. Colossians 1:21–22
24. Hebrews 10:17

3

APPROVAL ADDICT

"PLEASE DON'T REJECT ME"

The bell rang twenty seconds ago at Washington High. Jared is already in the hallway starting his longest walk of the day from the "C" wing of the school to the cafeteria. If he rushes, he can make it in two minutes. But the food this school serves gives him no motivation to rush anywhere. Jared isn't thinking about what's on the menu for lunch, or what his history teacher just said about the Civil War, or what his grade point average is, or what his mother told him this morning. His mind is focused on one question as he walks past the crowds gathering outside each classroom. He sees their eyes glancing back and forth at him and asks himself, *What do they think about me?*

Jennifer is rushing (almost running) from the "A" wing to the cafeteria, not for the food either. In fact, she probably won't eat anything more than a couple of chips and a bite of yogurt all day.

She is worried about being fat. She bolts through the cafeteria door to get a spot at the long table where she and her "friends" from the cool crowd sit, swap gossip, roll their eyes, and laugh about the poor losers in their morning classes. Tenth grade has been great for Jennifer so far because these girls have invited her into their tight group. This is the group you want to be in. But she still rushes to the cafeteria every day because, deep down, she fears that if all the seats at the table are taken before she gets there, nobody will make a place for her—then she will be stuck sitting at a table with the pitiful losers that the group loves to mock.

If you beamed a mind-scanner into the halls of WHS (or your school, too), the words that appear most often would be: "What are all these other people thinking about me?" "Am I cool?" "Am I funny?" "Am I attractive?"

How hard is it to crack the secret of popularity? It doesn't take too long in most schools to figure it out. Ask yourself these questions:

⇒ Do people want to sit next to me? Or do they move away when I sit down?

⇒ Have I ever heard anyone bragging about being *my* friend?

⇒ When I talk about my weekend plans, do people ask if they can come, too?

Admit it, those questions and fears flash like lightning in our brains. This game started back in elementary school, but it gets more serious every year. Most of us have walked the halls with a fantasy playing in our minds. We dream that we have done something—traveled to a European country, met someone famous, scored a winning point—that would impress everyone, that would change everything. We imagine walking past all those open lockers feeling confident, even cocky, knowing that we were popular and somebody worth knowing. Then reality snaps back and we find ourselves where we normally are every day—feeling inferior, afraid, and a little sad about who we really are.

But the fantasy keeps coming back—weekly, daily, even hourly—because we want to feel good about ourselves in comparison to our peers. So we ask ourselves, "What am I willing to do to hear other people say I'm cool?"

When asked what they would like to change most about themselves, teenagers usually answer by naming something about their physical appearance. Why are so many people unhappy with their physical appearance?

What would you like to change about yourself?

AM I OKAY?

All this insecurity and inferiority is a disease in our system. Even the most successful people have ongoing struggles with insecurity. They feel the pressure to keep "performing" to get the approval of others and feel good about who they are.

This insecurity, inferiority, and fear of rejection come automatically when we enter the world. They're the result of Adam and Eve's sin and our broken relationship with God. Satan exploits our insecurities and gets us to play the comparison game with our friends. We wonder if we're cool because we don't feel okay. Something is missing. We need assurance from somewhere; someone to tell us we are respected and to let us know how we fit in this world.

> **Satan's Most Successful Lie:
> Self-Worth =
> Performance +
> Others' Opinions**

What makes all this a big deal is that our world is constantly telling us that being accepted and popular is the big test we have to pass to get a good life. Television commercials and magazine ads show young people having a good time dancing, drinking, and driving around with hip, cool people. We want to be there, too. So we take off on the quest to find a group where we will be accepted. The message gets hammered home—that getting the approval of others and comparing ourselves to our peers is the only reliable way to tell how we are doing on this awkward journey toward adulthood.

When we make these comparisons it can be painful and confusing. So many people look stronger or more beautiful. They are smarter, more athletic, and more talented than what we see in ourselves. We immediately jump to the only logical conclusion: "I'm not as good as the cool kids in my school." Or maybe we decide that we're better than the other people we go to school with; we're cooler than them. When we compare ourselves to others, we never win. We are either totally down on ourselves, depressed; or we're stuck up and conceited, better than everyone else.

Day after day we judge ourselves and believe that big lie: *There's something wrong with me. If only I could change* _____. Every day, layers of inferiority and self-hate wrap around us. They squeeze the fun and joy out of our teen years. It discourages us from exploring who we really are and developing the talent and abilities God has given us.

Think About This. "I trust in God. I will not be afraid. What can people do to me?"[1] Think of a time when you wouldn't try a new activity or new challenge because you were afraid of what others would think about you. What was it, and how did it turn out?

If we could take a trip to our future high-school reunion twenty years from now, we would find that what we want so badly right now isn't going to be that important when we get older. The inferiority we feel now is so phony because it is based on good looks or athletic ability or getting the right boyfriend. The people we think are so "it" have the same fears and insecurities we do. They are scared of failing and being rejected. They just cover it up with their popularity, good looks, and athletic talent and pretend to have it all together.

Twenty years from now we will realize how foolish it was to try to win their approval so we could feel good about ourselves. How dumb to let our self-worth and value be determined by what they thought of us! But now it's hard to see that and believe it. You don't want to be in the dork group at your school. You want to be popular, have friends, and have fun.

Rejection hurts. We've seen kids get rejected ever since kindergarten. They get left out at recess or sit alone on the bus. They have no one to talk to or walk home with. People talk about them behind their backs and laugh at them to their faces. They retreat into their private worlds of video games or music, sometimes even depression or repressed anger. They go through school alone or find other friends who carry similar hurts. Life doesn't feel so good.

That fear is so real that we are willing to do almost anything to keep it from happening to us. How strong is that fear of rejection and desire to fit in with others who you decide are cool?

Living according to the false belief that you *must be approved by certain others to feel good about yourself* causes you to fear rejection, making you willing to change your attitudes and actions to match the expectations of others. This self-test will help make you aware of how sensitive you are to the threat of rejection.

What will you see in those results? Is the fear of rejection a strong feeling that you have when you are trying to make decisions? Does the fear of rejection dominate your mind and contribute to loneliness and a withdrawal from other people? Have rejection experiences caused you to dislike yourself?

POP QUIZ

Rate yourself according to each of the following statements. Be as honest as possible.

1
When I sense that someone might reject me, I become nervous and anxious.
Never ... 1 ... 2 ... 3 ... 4 ... 5 ... 6 ... 7 ... 8 ... 9 ... 10 ... Always

2
I am uncomfortable around those who are different from me.
Never ... 1 ... 2 ... 3 ... 4 ... 5 ... 6 ... 7 ... 8 ... 9 ... 10 ... Always

3
I am critical of others.
Never ... 1 ... 2 ... 3 ... 4 ... 5 ... 6 ... 7 ... 8 ... 9 ... 10 ... Always

4 I find myself trying to impress others.

Never ...1 ...2 ...3 ...4 ...5 ...6 ...7 ...8 ...9 ...10 ... Always

5 I always try to determine what people think of me.

Never ...1 ...2 ...3 ...4 ...5 ...6 ...7 ...8 ...9 ...10 ... Always

Add up your total score.

Interpreting the Results

If your score was:

61–70: Congratulations! You are virtually free from the fear of rejection. You have a healthy view of yourself as accepted and loved by God. (Maybe *you* should be writing this chapter!)

41–60: Good! You have a very small fear of rejection. It may be only certain situations that cause you trouble. However, it is likely that a good number of your decisions are made to minimize your chance of being rejected. You should take note of the ideas in this chapter about your acceptance coming from God, not friends or parents.

21–40: You have a high fear of rejection. Your emotional lows will almost always be a result of your fear of rejection, or the belief that you have already been rejected in some way. Nearly all of your decisions are designed to help you win the approval of others.

0–20: You have an overwhelming fear of rejection. Experiences of rejection fill your memories. You probably have feelings of depression often. If this is the case, you should talk to a parent or counselor to see about having someone to walk with you so you can overcome this fear.

NOTE: If you ended up with a score that is lower than you'd prefer, don't panic. This "test" isn't the final word on your life. It's just a snapshot of where you happen to be right now. Nearly everyone has struggled (or does struggle) with the fear of rejection to some degree. But God doesn't want us to spend our lives seeking the approval of others. The rest of this chapter will guide you through God's awesome solution for freeing people from the fear of rejection.

HOW FEAR OF REJECTION MESSES YOU UP

Fear of rejection lies to you.
It tells you that you don't measure up to some standard that has been created or adopted. It is a tool of manipulation designed to control someone. It is expressed with an outburst of anger, a disgusted look, an impatient answer, or a social snub. It communicates disrespect, inferior value, and lack of appreciation. Rejection hurts.

Fear of rejection is used to manipulate you.
You know people who change their behavior to avoid being rejected by someone important to them. Even misguided pastors

and religious leaders use fear of rejection and guilt to get people to respond to a message, give money, or work in the service of the church. Any person in a position of authority can use this manipulative pressure to get someone to do what will serve their temporary desires and goals.

Fear of rejection leads some people into isolation.

They become loners, not getting too close to the people in their life or even staying away from people completely. After experiencing rejection from family or romantic relationships, it is too big a risk to open their lives to other people who might reject them yet again in the future.

Fear of rejection makes you reject others.

A person who has felt the sting of rejection should understand how much it hurts others. But instead, the same judgment and comparison on the basis of outward appearance and performance that hurt you so badly are often brutally poured out on others who don't fit the mold.

Fear of rejection makes you give in.

It causes some people to continually say yes to everyone and everything in order to gain their affection and approval. They find themselves overcommitted and taken advantage of by leaders or friends. On the outside they are the most helpful and reliable people, but on the inside they can be resentful and angry yet unable to say no because of the fear that they will be disliked or rejected.

> Our fear of rejection controls us to the degree by which we base our self-worth on the opinions of others. We become slaves to how we think others see us. In what ways do you feel like a slave to the opinions of other people?

SYMPTOMS OF THE FEAR OF REJECTION

Rejection can trigger serious problems in our lives. No problem comes from only one source, but this list of problems is often the product of an unhealthy fear of rejection. These problems are best addressed by contacting a professional spiritual leader, counselor, or therapist. The following is a partial list of the problems related to this fear of rejection.

Anger, Resentment, Hostility

Anger is the most common response to rejection. Many times we are not honest about our anger. We are afraid to express our anger to certain people in our lives. What they think about us is so important to us that we bottle up our anger and become resentful and politely hostile (being sarcastic toward them, avoiding them, etc.). Eventually this blows up in a destructive pattern of living or becomes a deep resentment. Unless we address our fear of rejection and change our responses to the people who trigger this reaction in us, we will not live healthy lives.

Being Easily Manipulated

People who believe that their self-worth is based on the approval of others are likely to do almost anything to please others. Obviously this is very dangerous. It opens people up to drug use, alcohol abuse, and sexual promiscuity.

Codependency

In families where one (or more) members are addicted to alcohol, drugs, work, or any other compulsion, other family members often develop the desire to rescue the addicted person from the consequences of his or her behavior. This feeling that you need to rescue the other person is called codependency. It allows the cycle of destructive behavior to continue.

Control

In an effort to avoid being hurt, some people constantly try to maintain control of others and dominate the situations they face.

They become skilled in exercising control by sending messages of approval or disapproval, unwilling to let others be themselves and make their own decisions. Such people are actually insecure and the lack of control is a threat to them.

Negative Self-Talk

When other people tell you negative things about yourself, and you dwell on them, think about them over and over, that is negative self-talk. It is the messages of disapproval from others that hurt the *most* that we repeat to ourselves. Even long after the comment has been made—the person may even have passed away—we continue to repeat the negative, hurtful messages.

Hypersensitivity to Opinions of Others

Worrying how others will react to what we do or say (especially when we anticipate a negative response) makes it difficult to make good decisions. Instead of acting positively and moving forward, we believe the worst about how others might react. We condemn ourselves to failure before we even get started.

GOD'S SOLUTION FOR THE APPROVAL ADDICT

It was never God's desire to see us living in fear—feeling threatened by other human beings and wondering what is wrong with us. Our broken relationship with God and sin's presence in our lives brings the hurt we experience from being rejected by others. In our desperation we lash out and do exactly the same to others. But God has an answer for our separation from Him and all the negative ways it affects our life.

God offers us total and complete acceptance, with no performance demands and no threats of rejection. God provides *reconciliation*, which means He accepts everyone who is willing to come to Him, including those *we* might think are unacceptable (because of their reputation or what they have done). He even welcomes those who condemn themselves and believe they are unacceptable to God.

Jesus gave special attention and time to Zacchaeus, the corrupt tax collector whom everybody hated.[2] He had felt the rejection of others, perhaps because he was so short. Maybe it was because he was making a living working for the enemy (the Roman Empire), or because he was really good at cheating people out of their money. Whatever the reason (or maybe it was all of them), people hated him.

Zacchaeus made those mistakes, there's no doubt about that. But that didn't mean God couldn't love him. Jesus knew about every one of those bad marks on Zacchaeus's record, but He knew his true value in God's sight and loved him in spite of all the evil he had done. Jesus ate dinner at Zacchaeus's house, and the time He spent with him changed that cheating tax collector's life. When he finally understood that he was accepted and loved by God, he immediately gave away half of his money to needy people. (Remember that he placed all his identity in the money he made. This money was what he was hoping would make him important and powerful.) He also repaid people he had cheated four times the amount he had taken from them.

What caused this huge change in a man that everyone hated? He found out from Jesus that God loved him unconditionally and accepted him completely. He realized that his life was valuable and significant to God. Jesus showed him that God was his friend, not his enemy.

Reconciliation means that those who were enemies have become friends. We were at odds with God because we share in Adam and Eve's sin. Just like them we have tried to live our lives without God—like we were smarter than Him and knew what was best for us. But God showed great mercy and love to us when He sent Christ to die on the cross. His death was not for just the people who are good and nice. His death was to pay for the sins of the very worst people as well—even those who are ungrateful and far away from God. The unconditional acceptance we get from Christ is a profound, life-changing truth. This is not just a ticket to heaven but the beginning of a whole new relationship with God.

Our worth lies in the fact that Christ's blood has paid for our sins; therefore, we are reconciled to God. We are accepted on that basis alone. How do you feel when you know that God accepts you completely?

WHAT RECONCILIATION IS ALL ABOUT

The last chapter explained that *justification* is the Bible word that describes how we were declared "not guilty" in God's sight because of the forgiveness and righteousness of Christ. *Reconciliation* (another good Bible term) explains the kind of relationship God wants to have with us. To be reconciled with someone means that whatever we have done in the past has been forgiven and forgotten. God adopts us into His family and makes us joint heirs with Christ. Everything that belongs to God will someday be given to us. God gives us His unbreakable word and promise.

If these religious words are confusing, just think of the picture Jesus told in the story about the prodigal son and his loving father.[3] Jesus told the people about a son who rebelled, moved away from his family, and wasted all his money on wild, "Real World Cancun" living. But when he came to his senses and decided to return home, his father didn't shun him or reject him. The father ran to meet him and welcomed him back! The son had planned to ask his father if he could live at his house as a servant, because he was sure that he had forever blown his chance to be a son. But the father threw a huge party celebrating the newfound life of this lost son that he thought was dead.

Can you imagine God loving you that much and completely accepting you no matter what you have done in the past? When someone loves you like that, you don't care what others say about you. You are certainly not afraid of being rejected by strangers because you have secure status with Almighty God, who created you and wants to live at the center of your life.

RECONCILIATION IS FOR EVERYONE

The apostle Paul was totally forgiven and accepted by God after he persecuted and killed people because they were Christians. He said this reconciliation, this change of relationship with God, is possible because of what Christ did for us on the cross:

> At one time you were separated from God. You were his enemies in your minds, and the evil things you did were against God. But now God has made you his friends again. He did this through Christ's death in the body so that he might bring you into God's presence as people who are holy, with no wrong, and with nothing of which God can judge you guilty.[4]

Through Christ's death on the cross we have become acceptable to God. It wasn't because God forgot or overlooked our mistakes and sins. It happened because Jesus gave His life to save us by paying the penalty for the sins that separated us from God.

The unconditional love of God changes people from the inside out. Here's how Paul described what happens to people who receive the gift God offers by putting their faith in Christ:

If anyone belongs to Christ, there is a new creation. The old things have gone; everything is made new! All this is from God. Through Christ, God made peace between us and himself, and God gave us the work of telling everyone about the peace we can have with him.[5]

THE BIGGEST CHOICE IN LIFE

This is the biggest choice we will ever make in our lives. It determines how we understand who we are and what our life is all about. We can either listen to popular culture tell us what is cool and base our self-worth on the approval of others, or we can listen and respond to what God has said and done for us. When we understand and believe what Jesus did for us and ask Him to be our Lord and Savior, it's not just about getting to heaven. It means finding acceptance and security with God that can never be taken away so that we can be set free every minute of the day.

Ethan is one of thousands of teenagers who have been set free by the reality of unconditional love from God. Ethan never felt loved or secure growing up in a broken home. The rejection he felt from his father, his teachers, and his peers made him constantly angry. He rejected everyone who tried to help him and his mom. He frustrated professional counselors and therapists with his agitating and angering behavior.

A breakthrough came when he met a Christian counselor who willingly absorbed all the abuse Ethan could give out. The counselor talked about God's unconditional love, week after week. Ethan's increasing anger provoked him to do everything he could to knock the counselor off his case.

The time came when Ethan finally understood that God loved him for who he was as God saw him, and not according to what he had done in the past. He had failed many times, but in God's eyes he wasn't a failure. Grasping that unconditional love promised by God opened Ethan's life for some major changes in attitude and actions, based on his new awareness of God's total and complete acceptance of him.

REJECTING THE LIES AND FEAR

Other people can help you experience God's truth. Some learn the truth about God from their own parents, but many grow up in homes with parents who aren't good role models. Instead, they grow up surrounded by neglect, condemnation, and manipulation. Others have even deeper wounds of sexual abuse, physical abuse, and abandonment. If your parents don't fit the description of "good role models," you should get to know other people—Christian friends and counselors—who will demonstrate God's love, forgiveness, and power. The deep wounds can begin to heal and a Christlike character will start to form in your life.

If you need to experience God's love reborn and rebuilt in you, you may need to find a pastor or counselor who can help you get started. Being honest and open about the wounds in your life is a dangerous, wild place to be. All the securities of your masks are gone, and people will see you for who you really are. But in God's love, sharing your life with a small group of friends can be a place for comfort and encouragement.

Ask God for guidance and be open to reading and applying His Word. Don't be afraid to take risks. Be open to change. God will bring people into your life who can help you cultivate healthy relationships.

RECAP

Our self-worth lies in the fact that Christ's blood has paid for our sins, making it possible for us to be reconciled to God. We are completely and totally accepted on that basis alone. We are totally accepted by God, who made us and knows us best of all. Without this approval from Him, our self-worth depends on what our friends, culture, and parents say, and how we measure up to what they expect of us. Not to mention what we expect of ourselves!

Living in fear of other people's opinions produces serious emotional and relational problems. But living in the confidence of God's unchanging opinion of us gives us the freedom to develop the gifts He gives us, without worrying that He will reject us.

DO THIS

Reconciliation is the greatest theme of the Bible.

⇒ Read each of the following passages taken from the Bible on the topic of reconciliation.

⇒ Answer the question that follows each passage.

⇒ Meditate on these words. Allow God to speak to you as you read His Word.

⇒ Memorize as many of these passages as possible. They will be the foundation for finding your true significance.

He has taken our sins away from us as far as the east is from the west.[6]
What happens to the mistakes you make?

This is my blood which is the new agreement that God makes with his people. This blood is poured out for many to forgive their sins.[7]
Why did Christ die for you?

God loved the world so much that he gave his one and only Son so that whoever believes in him may not be lost, but have eternal life.[8]

What is God's promise to you?

I tell you the truth, whoever hears what I say and believes in the One who sent me has eternal life. That person will not be judged guilty but has already left death and entered life.[9]

Why do you think God promised you this great gift?

All have sinned and are not good enough for God's glory, and all need to be made right with God by his grace, which is a free gift. They need to be made free from sin through Jesus Christ.[10]

What is your favorite thing about being made right with God?

Happy are they whose sins are forgiven.[11]

When are you happiest?

While we were God's enemies, he made friends with us through the death of his Son. Surely, now that we are his friends, he will save us through his Son's life.[12]

Do you consider God to be your friend?

The Spirit we received does not make us slaves again to fear; it makes us children of God. With that Spirit we cry out, "Father."[13]

Describe your relationship with God.

Yes, I am sure that neither death, nor life, nor angels, nor ruling spirits, nothing now, nothing in the future, no powers, nothing above us, nothing below us, nor anything else in the whole world will ever be able to separate us from the love of God that is in Christ Jesus our Lord.[14]

Why is Paul so convinced?

If anyone belongs to Christ, there is a new creation. The old things have gone; everything is made new! . . . God was in Christ, making peace between the world and himself. In Christ, God did not hold the world guilty of its sins. And he gave us this message of peace. . . . Christ had no sin, but God made him become sin so that in Christ we could become right with God.[15]

Describe why your identity in Christ is so important.

In Christ we are set free by the blood of his death, and so we have forgiveness of sins. How rich is God's grace.[16]

How do you experience God's grace?

I mean that you have been saved by grace through believing. You did not save yourselves; it was a gift from God. It was not the result of your own efforts, so you cannot brag about it.[17]

Do you feel proud that God saved you?

Let us look only to Jesus, the One who began our faith and who makes it perfect. He suffered death on the cross. But he accepted the shame as if it were nothing because of the joy that God put before him. And now he is sitting at the right side of God's throne.[18]

How is faith made perfect?

Praise be to the God and Father of our Lord Jesus Christ. In God's great mercy he has caused us to be born again into a living hope, because Jesus Christ rose from the dead. Now we hope for the blessings God has for his children. These blessings, which cannot be destroyed or be spoiled or lose their beauty, are kept in heaven for you.[19]

What blessings are in heaven for you?

Allow God to speak to you as you read His Word and answer these questions. Doing this will help you build your self-worth on a solid, unchanging foundation.

VERSES TO READ:

1. Psalm 56:11
2. Luke 19:1–10
3. Luke 15:11–32
4. Colossians 1:21–22
5. 2 Corinthians 5:17–18
6. Psalm 103:12
7. Matthew 26:28
8. John 3:16
9. John 5:24
10. Romans 3:23–24

11. Romans 4:7
12. Romans 5:10
13. Romans 8:15
14. Romans 8:38–39
15. 2 Corinthians 5:17, 19, 21
16. Ephesians 1:7
17. Ephesians 2:8–9
18. Hebrews 12:2
19. 1 Peter 1:3–4

4

BLAME AND CONDEMNATION

"THE BLAME GAME"

Do you walk through metal detectors when you enter your school? Many use scanning machines to keep weapons out. Yet every day, students and teachers alike enter their schools packing a concealed deadly weapon that goes undetected by the x-ray machines. It is so lethal it can wound, maim, or change the life of its victim forever.

I carry this weapon with me everywhere I go. I think you do, too. It's our ability to send a message of condemnation or blame to another person using words, physical force, facial expressions, or silence. When fired, this weapon can reverberate with loud explosions of harsh physical or verbal abuse, or it may go almost undetected with muffled thuds of sarcasm, shunning, or rejection. This weapon is very personal. We use it for defensive and offensive purposes. Whatever circumstances motivate us to use it, we are confident it will deliver a powerful and destructive message to those who challenge us: "I'll make you sorry for what you did."

It's also open warfare in our schools and homes. We are as likely to be hit as we are to pull the trigger. The weapons of condemnation and blame are aimed at those who fail. We've all stared down its barrel of condemnation and blame. We have the scars to prove it. Life has taught us: *Those who fail are unworthy of love and deserve to be punished.*

COLOSSAL FAILURE

Matt made a stupid mistake when he was fourteen that he is still paying for. He and several friends tried to slip past the security guard at the music store with some CDs they didn't pay for. They got snagged at the door and were hauled back to the manager's office.

Matt has not heard the end of it. It's been five years, but his father reminds him constantly (with sarcasm and verbal jabs) that he is a liar and a thief. Anytime Matt's grades or behavior comes in below his dad's expectations, his father fires away, "You're a failure and an embarrassment to this family. You'll never amount to anything."

Matt isn't able to forget the humiliation that his father has dished out to him. Now at nineteen, he tells a counselor that he has a hard time being happy for very long. He'll be somewhere enjoying himself until he realizes he is feeling good. Then a depressed feeling comes over him because something inside tells him he is worthless and has no right to feel good about himself.

What mistakes have you made in the past that your parents or friends keep bringing up to make you feel bad?

Like so many people, Matt has been peppered by blasts of condemnation and blame. He's been wounded and infected with the false belief that *those who fail are unworthy of love and deserve to be punished.*

TARGETS OF CONDEMNATION AND BLAME

We all fail. That makes us easy targets for blame. None of us measure up to the standards our culture pushes for beauty, talent, intelligence, popularity, or success. The images on TV and in magazines make us look and feel like losers.

This is where life gets real nasty and serious. Growing up isn't much fun when someone is blaming you for their problems or judging you for your mistakes. Adults can sue for "libel" and "slander" when this happens to them, but there is little protection from this verbal assault if you are young. For many of us, condemnation and blame have been coming at us since we were kids. Then, when you hit middle school, there was a huge spike in cruel words and social rejection. While parents and pastors are concerned about the effects of watching excessive violence in movies and videos, no one seems to notice the burn of violent words and labels shot at you every day in real life by your parents or peers.

Life isn't fair. We all have different physical shapes that develop on nonpredictable schedules. We grow up in family situations so different from what other people our age experience. We try our best to fit in and be liked, but most of the time it seems as if other people got all the good stuff and we got stuck with the leftovers when God was putting the world together.

We start to believe the big lie: *Those who fail are not worthy of love and deserve to be punished.* So when we fail in front of our peers, they dole out the punishment. Their words and rejection sting us and stay with us for a long time.

Dan thinks it was sometime during the seventh grade when the kids in his school started calling him "Meatball." He laughs now and admits his body probably did resemble a huge meatball. For those months on the way to puberty he was a round mound of mostly fat and not much muscle. But the nickname stuck and stayed with him for years. Along with the name came an ugly feeling that bored a sense of inferiority deep into his soul. Years later, now living in a tall, muscular body, Dan says there are many days when he still feels like "Meatball"—the fat, ugly kid who was rejected and ridiculed by the cool kids at school.

What comments hurt you the most when you were a kid?

What have you said to others that was hurtful?

Today Dan realizes that on that playground years ago all the kids in his class felt the same fear of being rejected and ridiculed that he did. To cope, they switched into survival mode. Every man for himself. They hid behind each other and pointed their verbal weapons at the little fat kid, and pulled the trigger . . . day after day. Dan was an easy target. They kept the condemnation and blame away from their own fragile self-esteem by aiming the abuse at someone else.

FRIENDLY FIRE

But school isn't the only place you get hit by condemnation and blame. The military uses the term "friendly fire" when soldiers are shot by their own troops. Some of us have taken some significant friendly fire from the people we thought were on our side—our own family. Perhaps you have your own story (like Matt's) of how your mom or dad can't let go of some mistake you made. They turn a stupid mistake into a defining moment that tattoos who we are and what we are like. The more we hear blame and condemnation from our parents, the more we get clues of what they went through when they were teenagers. Have you ever thought of it that way?

Most often our parents pass on to us what was given to them when they were growing up. They shape our lives with the influences and ideas that were poured into them. When angry explosions or drugs and alcohol are in the house, it is hard to feel loved, accepted, and secure. But chances are, if your parents didn't get much verbal encouragement or support as kids, they probably don't know how to show it to you now. Unless something life-changing happens to them, they won't know how to break the cycle of blame and condemnation.

The main pressure some parents feel is to be successful in raising you—their child. They get mad and blame you when you make a mistake because, in their minds, their success as parents is tied to what you do. They are tempted to use manipulation to get you to do what they think will make them look like the most fantastic parents. When you don't meet their expectations or ful-fill the dreams they have for you, the double-barrel blast of blame hits you because they are trying to cover *their* feelings of failure.

Some of our parents are fighting the same battle of positive self-worth that we are. What we do with our lives is very impor-tant to them. They hope we grow up successful and attractive so they can brag about us and feel better in front of their peers. They may be living by the same lie we often are: *Those who fail are unworthy of love and deserve to be punished.*

Michael failed. He walked out during his SAT exam last fall. He was frustrated and overwhelmed that morning. School had never been easy for him. He spent the rest of the day helping a contractor build a swimming pool, which was fun. When he told his dad that night, his dad exploded in anger at dinner. He'd spent the last twenty years working hard and saving money so that everyone in the family would graduate from college. How could Michael not even finish the test? Was he stupid?

According to his father, Michael was ruining his future and the reputation of their college-educated family because he preferred running backhoes and cement mixers to memorizing vocabulary words. His parents are giving him the silent treatment these days. They stopped arguing with Michael about the importance of college and his future. But the silence between them is really loud. The message Michael hears in the silence is that he is a big disappointment, a failure, to his parents.

The way our parents live puts thoughts and ideas in our brain that stay there for a long time. We learn this lifestyle from them, and we will pass it on to our own families in the future. We must look carefully at our lives, and see what it is we truly believe and want to pass on, or these false beliefs will influence our feelings and actions and our responses to life. Unless we have a breakthrough experience that exposes the deadly lies and opens us up to the truth about who we are, we could injure many people we love with these same weapons of blame and condemnation.

IT'S MY FAULT

Life gets even more messed up when we turn these weapons on ourselves. In this culture of blame, everybody's looking for a culprit, but condemnation and blame become lethal when used on ourselves. Life is filled with dips and curves. It shakes us up. When we make mistakes we wonder what is wrong and who is to blame. When we can't find the answer, sometimes we start assuming the problem must be rooted in who we are and what we have done. Remember: "Those who fail (especially me) are unworthy of love and deserve to be punished."

Sarah failed. Her parents are divorced today, and she's convinced it is her fault. When she was eleven, she stayed at a friend's house past her curfew. Her mom called the house to say she was driving over to pick up Sarah and her bike. Not wanting to get in trouble with her mom for staying so late, Sarah told her friend to tell her mom she had already left (when she called) and was on her way home. Trying to hurry, Sarah was riding on the wrong side of the street and didn't see the car coming around the corner. The crash put Sarah in a body cast and in the hospital for three months. Her mom quit her job and was there at the hospital day and night the whole time.

When Sarah came home, the months that followed were filled with tension. Her dad was working a second job to pay the enormous medical bills. He and her mom argued about money and never spent any time together. Almost a year to the day of her accident her dad moved out of the house. That was four years ago, but last week Sarah overheard her aunt telling her grandmother something that Sarah has always told herself was true. Her aunt said if Sarah had been home on time that night, the accident and all the trouble that followed, including the divorce, would never have happened.

Self-condemnation is a severe form of punishment. Too many of us operate on the theory that if we punish ourselves enough, then God will not have to punish us. The greater the guilt, the longer and deeper the self-condemnation. Some people spend their whole life punishing themselves for what happened in their family—over which they had little or no control.

What is in your life now, or from your past, that keeps condemning you?

What do you have a hard time forgiving yourself for?

Remember, our fear of punishment comes from the false belief that says, *Those who fail (especially me) are unworthy of love and deserve to be punished.* How much does this false belief manipulate and control you? One way to find out is to take this pop quiz.

Remember, this isn't a test that determines your future. It's more like a digital photo of where you are right now. It's a personal inventory—for your eyes only. You get to "grade" yourself and get a more accurate sense of how deeply you've been affected by wrong ideas about punishment and blame. Are you ready to be most honest with yourself?

POP QUIZ

Write the correct number in the blank next to each statement.

1 = Always
2 = Very Often
3 = Often
4 = Sometimes
5 = Seldom
6 = Very Seldom
7 = Never

_____ 1. I fear what God might do to me.

_____ 2. When I fail, I worry about what God thinks of me.

_____ 3. When I see someone else suffering, I wonder what they did to deserve it.

_____ 4. When something goes wrong, I catch myself thinking that God must be punishing me for something I have done.

_____ 5. I am very hard on myself when I fail.

_____ 6. I catch myself wanting to blame people when they
fail.

_____ 7. I get angry with God when someone who is bad
gets rewarded with success.

_____ 8. When I see someone doing something wrong, I
have to tell them what I think of them.

_____ 9. I tend to focus on the faults and failures of others.

_____ 10. God seems harsh and judgmental to me.

_____ **TOTAL**

Interpreting the Results

If your score was:

57–70: Congratulations! You have a strong appreciation for God's
love and unconditional acceptance. You seem to be free
from the fear of punishment that plagues most people.

40–56: Good! You have a very small fear of punishment. It may be
only certain situations where fear of punishment controls
your responses to people. When you have emotional
problems, they may relate to a fear of punishment or an
inner urge to punish yourself or others.

25–39: You have a high fear of punishment. There are many days
in your life when you are strongly influenced by feelings of
punishment and blame. This robs you of the joy and peace
that God wants to give you.

0–24: Experiences of punishment dominate your memory and
have produced a good amount of depression and low self-

esteem in you. These feelings will continue to dominate you until you experience a deep healing in your self-concept based on God's forgiveness and unconditional love.

If you ended up with a score that is lower than you'd prefer, don't panic. The rest of this chapter will guide you through God's awesome solution for freeing people from the fear of punishment and blame.

LEARNING TO ACCEPT OURSELVES WHEN WE FAIL

Blame is the core of most emotional disturbances, according to some psychologists. They say that assigning blame to yourself for failure can have serious and damaging consequences. A number of emotional problems are rooted in the false belief that when we fail, the only way to deal with our shortcomings and mistakes is to punish ourselves and others for them. The answer, they say, is for each of us to stop blaming and learn to accept ourselves in spite of our imperfections.

Did you get that? The psychologists' answer is for each of us to just stop the self-condemnation and learn to accept ourselves with all our faults. Stop blaming others and forgive. That's simple, right? How many people have heard that advice and said, "If only it were that easy," and then walked right back into their life of bitterness, punishment, and fear?

When we grapple with what to believe about who we are and what life is all about, the stakes are high. It boils down to how we define success and failure. If we believe that what we do, how popular we are, and what other people think of us are the standards for "success," then we are going to feel okay about condemning those who fall short of that mark, including ourselves. We condemn ourselves, and then in an act of self-survival, we condemn others. That's why we feel so bad and empty at the same time. We can't even live up to our own standard of success, yet we're blasting others who make the same mistakes. We are all on the same sinking ship.

That's right—our ship is sinking. We need a rescue—someone to save us from this self-destructive spiral. We have felt the bullets of blame from peers, parents, and ourselves. Our parents give us what they got from their parents. We give it to our friends and peers. When they give it back to us, we turn around and slam this blame and condemnation on ourselves. It's a ricocheting bullet that eventually ends up killing our joy and optimism for life.

This cycle has to stop. By this point in this book I bet you can guess who we are counting on to come to our rescue. Even before I mention His name you may be thinking, *But He's the only One who has a legitimate reason to condemn us.* It doesn't take much to get us feeling guilty when someone mentions His name. Remember the lie: *Those who fail are unworthy of love and deserve to be punished?* Many people know they have failed, especially according to God's standards, and cannot imagine that God would give them anything but condemnation and blame.

Never grace or mercy. Mention God, and they instantly feel guilty.

HOW GOD HANDLES OUR FAILURE

God is holy. That means He is perfect in every way. In fact, God sets the standard for what is right and wrong. To be truly holy, God must punish those who sin. That translates into big trouble for all of us who are human. Up against God's standards, we are all failures and we are facing the punishment of God.

I can almost hear you saying, "See, I told you so! God does condemn me. So now I am really messed up. How can God rescue me from the cycle of blame if He is condemning me for not being perfect like Him?"

We're only human. We make mistakes all the time. Is it God's plan to make us feel bad about our failure so that we will punish ourselves and work harder and do more good things for Him? Is that what Christianity is all about?

THE HARD SIDE OF GOD

If you think the statement "We are facing the punishment of God" doesn't seem fair, you're not alone. People have been trying to get rid of their guilt by changing God's standards for a long time. Even churches have tried to soften these "hard" standards of God. It seems unfair that God would punish everyone who does not live perfectly according to His rules. They argue that because God is so big, powerful, and loving, His only reasonable response is to overlook some sins and give breaks to people who are, in general, someone you would call a "good person."

They want God to be like a teacher who grades on the curve. The pass-fail line is set according to how the rest of the class does on the test. In that system most people pass even though their scores are far less than perfect. But God's rules are different, and His Word says that only those who are perfect can be in heaven with God.

Do you see God more as condemning or forgiving?

What personal experiences have shaped your image of God?

This is the mysterious, justice-demanding character of God, but it is also the reason we can depend on Him and His Word. He does not change the rules to stay popular, and He doesn't allow us to make our own rules. To some people this seems too harsh and brutal for a God who is supposed to be full of love.

In reality, God has done way more than overlook our sins. He has erased them by sending Jesus Christ into our world to die on a cross. John, a much-loved disciple of Jesus, described what God did for us:

> This is how God showed his love to us: He sent his one and only Son into the world so that we could have life through him. This is what real love is: It is not our love for God; it is God's love for us in sending his Son to be the way to take away our sins. Dear friends, if God loved us that much we also should love each other.[1]

Because God is perfect, He requires justice. He can't just break the rules for us because He likes us. For Him to overlook one sin would pollute His holiness, like smearing a beautiful white dress with black tar.

We have offended God and His holiness with our sin. We broke the connection He created between us. We have ignored Him and broken His laws. Yet God is not just furious at our sin, He is also infinitely loving. He has provided for us what we could never do for ourselves. God didn't even wait for us to apologize or change our attitude before He sent Jesus to wipe out our debt. While we were still rebelling against God, Jesus

Christ came and died for us. Here's how Paul described what God did:

> Very few people will die to save the life of someone else. Although perhaps for a good person someone might possibly die. But God shows his great love for us in this way: Christ died for us while we were still sinners.
>
> So through Christ we will surely be saved from God's anger, because we have been made right with God by the blood of Christ's death. While we were God's enemies, he made friends with us through the death of his Son. Surely, now that we are his friends, he will save us through his Son's life. And not only that, but now we are also very happy in God through our Lord Jesus Christ. Through him we are now God's friends again.[2]

God's anger and wrath and His requirement for justice have been satisfied in the sacrifice of one perfectly innocent Man. Jesus' death on the cross appeased God and made amends with Him for the sins of everyone in the world. God provided it all for us.

WHAT GOD THINKS ABOUT US

This changes everything in our relationship with God. He is not waiting to pour out His blame and punishment on us. Our penalty has been paid by Christ. God now pours out His love and acceptance on us. He adopts us into a personal, intimate relationship with Him. Our status with God isn't based on the good things we do or how many mistakes we make. He loves us with a never-ending, unconditional love.

There is no doubt that God loves us. When our enemy, Satan, attacks us with blame for the mistakes we make and tells us we are no good, we have our own weapon to destroy those lies. We boldly tell our tempter that God sent Jesus Christ to pay for our sins. When we are full of fear and self-hate, we look at Jesus on the cross and know that the only reason He died there was because we are truly and deeply loved by God. We can measure our self-worth by what God thinks of us and what He has done so that our sins could be forgiven. God paid our debt in full.

Jesus said it clearly in John 3:17: "God did not send his Son into the world to judge the world guilty, but to save the world through him." He has removed all the condemnation and blame from every person who puts his or her faith and trust in Jesus Christ, God's Son. He also lets us know what happens when we trust in Him: "So if the Son makes you free, you will be truly free."[3]

The way God handles our failure is through forgiveness and total acceptance. If He can forgive all of our sins and accept us completely, then we can do the same for others and, most important, for ourselves.

HOW TO HANDLE OTHERS WHEN THEY HURT YOU

Not everybody in your school knows . . . or even cares . . . how much you are worth to God. They have their own fears of failure. To them you are just another competitor in a dog-eat-dog world. They do their best to wear a convincing mask of success. When they are overcome by fears of failure, they strike out at you. The more they knock you down the better they feel. They get their self-worth from being better than you are.

Remember when Dan's classmates started calling him "Meatball"? It kept the focus on Dan and all his physical and emotional shortcomings. So how does Dan ever get through this without intensely hating these kids or worse, yet, bringing a gun to school one day to settle the score? Or when Kara is harassed and called "nun" because she has decided to remain a virgin until she gets married, and Shaun is called "loser" because he let in the other team's winning goal, how do they keep a positive attitude? We have all been hurt by others—either by what they have said or done. Sometimes they mean to do it; many times they are blindly following the crowd or do it accidentally. Either way, it hurts. Once we understand what God thinks about us we have a solid place to start.

When we push Satan's lies out of our heads and let God's truth live inside us, we begin to gain confidence. We begin to understand and forgive those who blame us for ordinary stuff we do. Our worth isn't created or measured by what people think about our physical appearance, things we do, or even who we are. We have worth because God loves us. Anything else is a lie we have to get out of our heads.

When we replace those lies with God's truth about us and others—even those who may hurt and torment us—we become much healthier in our perspective. God loves them just as much as He loves us. And He still loves them when they are doing all that ugly junk to us.

This leads to three challenges that God gives us when we respond to those who hurt us. First, we should look at what we *want* to do to them when they hurt us. Am I looking for revenge? Do I gossip? Am I quick to forgive? Look at that response and compare it to what Christ does for you when you rebel against Him. When you do this, you will often discover that what you hate in them is rooted in your own behavior. But now, with Jesus, you are totally forgiven, and the Holy Spirit is working inside you, digging out sin and cutting it loose. Jesus said, "But I say to you who are listening, love your enemies. Do good to those who hate you, bless those who curse you, pray for those who are cruel to you."[4] Nothing anyone does to us can compare with our own sin and selfishness that have been completely forgiven by Christ.

Second, God challenges us not to blame others when they fail. Maybe they tried their best; perhaps they are just natural klutzes; maybe what they did hurt us directly or indirectly. Every day we see people fail. They don't need our biting blame chewing at them, too. They need our love and encouragement. Paul described clearly how God wants us to talk in Ephesians 4:29

when he said, "When you talk, do not say harmful things, but say what people need—words that will help others become stronger. Then what you say will do good to those who listen to you."

God wants to open our eyes so that we can see others struggling with their daily difficulties and flip the switch on our tongue from negative spewing (you know—blame and punish-

In what recent situation have you been with friends and heard someone being ridiculed or verbally abused?

How did you respond? What will you do in the future?

ment) to positive words (saying nice things).

Third, God has one job that He doesn't want us to do. He doesn't need us to speak for Him. We may be completely right in recognizing that what someone else is doing is wrong, but our job is *not* to hand out the punishment. Judgment is God's responsibility alone. Remember the story of the woman caught in adultery and brought to Jesus by an angry mob? The men there wanted to stone her. Jesus asked if any of those men were without sin. If so, they could throw the first stone. One by one they all walked away.

Over two thousand years later, Jesus stands beside you in the hallway of your school, on the athletic field, or at home, reminding you through His Spirit that throwing stones of blame and punishment is not your job. He challenges you to give love and affirmation even to the people who hurt you.

HOW TO HANDLE OUR OWN FAILURES

Most of us are harder on ourselves than anyone else could ever be. We know the truth about who we really are, our bad habits and our long list of failures. So when it is time to get hammered, we know how to bash ourselves better than anyone else.

Here's a big surprise! We all know that God wants to change our lives and make us better people, make us more like Him. But we often misunderstand that God's life-changing power in us is a *lifelong* process. God works in us even when we fail.

Matt became a Christian a month ago at a winter camp weekend. Never in his wildest dreams did he imagine how much knowing Jesus would fill the emptiness in his life. Still, he had a price to pay. His old friends have been all over him with plenty of jokes about this new faith, and a few days ago he really snapped. Standing in the halls after school, one of his friends accidentally slammed a locker door on Matt's fingers. It hurt so badly. The cusswords were flying out of Matt's mouth like no one had heard for a whole month since the winter camp. Ten minutes later, when Matt and all the guys walked out into the parking lot, some of them were already making a big deal about what happened.

This whole week Matt has been extremely quiet and even depressed. He feels like he really blew it when his mouth exploded. Now his friends will never believe that Jesus changed his life. In those painful moments by the lockers he sounded just like the old Matt. Maybe that's who he still is. Christians don't mess up like that, do they? Now he is thinking he really isn't worthy of God's love. Worse yet, he thinks, he deserves God's punishment. Those who fail are unworthy of love and deserve to be punished, right?

If you were Matt's friend, what would you tell him about his dilemma?

A big lesson any Christian (and especially a new Christian) must learn is how to respond to failure. The thoughts that flooded Matt's mind after the verbal explosion were *You are a failure as a Christian. Your friends will never believe you now. You'll never change; you'll always be the same old Matt.* But these messages of blame and condemnation don't come from God. They come from the enemy and are designed to make you feel unworthy of God's forgiveness and unconditional love.

Failure comes to all of us in big and small ways virtually every day, with the all-too familiar messages that Matt experienced. The good news is that a Christian can respond to failure by recognizing the sin, being sorry for it, and knowing that God forgives him or her.

John, in the Bible, declares that God, through Christ, has made a provision for all of us who fail:

> If we say we have no sin, we are fooling ourselves, and the truth is not in us. But if we confess our sins, he will forgive our sins, because we can trust God to do what is right. He will cleanse us from all the wrongs we have done.[5]

When we trust Christ to be our Savior, God has forgiven us of all our sins (past, present, and future). He wants us to experience His forgiveness every day—especially on days when we explode in blame and judgment. It's not the end of our relationship with Jesus Christ—although that is what Satan tries to tell us. The heroes of the Bible—like Moses, David, and Peter—made bad mistakes, but God forgave them completely. They picked themselves up, forgave themselves (because God forgave them), and moved forward to even greater responsibilities for God's kingdom.

Our failures and weaknesses don't threaten our self-worth or our relationship with God. God is the One who forgives us so that we can forgive ourselves and then forgive others. Growing through our failures and learning firsthand that God keeps His promises helps us mature and grow closer to Him. Our perception of God changes dramatically when we are confident that His grace covers all our mistakes.

Matt hasn't blown his chance to be a witness to his friends. Now he has an even clearer picture of God's message of salvation by grace (what Jesus did for us) and not works (what we try to do). Through Matt's real-life faith, his friends will learn that God isn't looking for perfect people. They don't exist. Instead, Jesus came to save those who will trust in Him and His death on the cross. They will learn from Matt that they cannot earn or pay for a relationship with God. It has already been paid in full.

RECAP

Just about everyone struggles with the issues of blame and condemnation. We hear those hurtful words from other people, even parents and friends. They make us feel unworthy of love and guilty for what we have done. Worst of all, we believe the lie that we cannot be loved or forgiven and convince ourselves that it is true.

But God sends us an entirely different message. He not only tells us that He loves and forgives us, He also demonstrated it in the most dramatic moment in history. He sacrificed His own Son, Jesus, so that our sins against God and the punishment we deserve could be taken care of. The Bible calls it *propitiation;* Jesus' death was the propitiation for our sins.

Receiving God's forgiveness frees us from condemnation. It also gives us the real opportunity to forgive others and ourselves. We can break the cycle of blame and condemnation because of what Jesus Christ did for us on the cross.

MIND RENEWAL EXERCISES

We need daily reminders that God has forgiven us. Here's one you can make to carry with you every day. On a card or paper write these words:

> Because of Christ and His death on the cross, I am completely forgiven and fully pleasing to God. I am forgiven and accepted by God.

Below that statement, copy the words of Romans 5:1 and Colossians 1:21–22. Then on the other side of the card write in big letters:

> God, help me today to accept and forgive myself as You have

accepted and forgiven me. Help me also to accept and forgive other people today (even people I don't like) in the same way that You forgive and accept me.

Keep this card with you so you can be reminded often. Let God's Word and your understanding of God's love for you change the way you look at and treat yourself and others.

VERSES TO READ:

1. 1 John 4:9–11
2. Romans 5:7–11
3. John 8:36
4. Luke 6:27–28
5. 1 John 1:8–9

5

SHAME

"I'LL NEVER CHANGE"

A glass mayonnaise jar sat empty on a tall wooden stool at the front of the camp assembly hall. Looking out at the 150 students sitting on the floor, the camp speaker began to fill the jar with pitcher after pitcher of water. In less than two hours all these teenagers would get on the buses to go home after six of the best days of their lives. Camp had been better than ever. For many of the students, this was the week that Jesus Christ had become real to them.

Now they were going home, "back to reality" somebody had said at breakfast. These were normal, average kids. That meant at least half of them would walk through the front door and have only one parent to greet them. Even though many of the students had made new commitments to be followers of Jesus Christ at camp, nothing had changed at home. The mood in the house, the pressure from friends, the television and radio shows hadn't changed while they had been away for the last six days.

It took eight pitchers of water to fill the mayonnaise jar. This was the industrial (camp size) container from which a lot of tuna salad mix had been made during the week. The camp speaker had obviously rescued it from the Dumpster. The label was partially torn off, but he had washed the inside sparkling clean.

But it didn't stay clean. With no explanation, the speaker began dumping ugly, nasty stuff into the container—used cooking grease, dirty motor oil, leftover beef gravy, ashes from last night's cookout, and even handfuls of dirt. The once–clear water became dark and cloudy. He dipped out a cup full of this new concoction from the jar and offered it to a girl in the front row. She gagged and pushed it away.

"This is your life," the speaker began. "God gave each of us a unique body and mind designed to hold all the truth, love, joy, and peace that He wanted to give us. But instead of our lives being full of God and stuff that comes from Him, our lives have been filled with ugly, nasty lies. Satan has used all sorts of things to pollute our minds and ruin the purity of our lives. When we are brave enough to look into our own hearts, we see the truth about how Satan has dramatically twisted and destroyed what God created to be good and pure, holy and righteous—just like Him. We were built to be free, but we have become slaves. We were created to be pulsating with life, but now we are gripped by fear, unhappiness, and even thoughts of self-destruction. What God created to be beautiful is now a murky mess."

Sarah sat totally silent listening to the speaker, but her heart was pounding inside. This had been the best week of her life. At camp she had made new friends and had had so much fun. The atmosphere was so different from home. People here accepted you and loved you for who you really were. By Wednesday she had stopped trying to impress people or manipulate them to give her attention. For the first time in a long time she could try new activities, like the ropes course or kayaking, and not be afraid that she would look foolish. This week she could shrug off the moments of failure and just try again. Her friends and her counselor gave her encouragement and helped her overcome her fears.

What thoughts have you had this week that are pleasing to God, and which ones are polluted?

What a week it had been! She had learned to pray—really pray. Not just the memorized prayers at meals and bedtime, but real words with real feelings. What the camp speaker had said was true—you could express your emotions and feelings to God and talk to Him like a real person. Sarah had never felt so free and alive.

Now it was all coming to an end. The buses would tear her

away from her friends. Her counselor's kind and encouraging voice would be replaced by her mother's negative accusations. Sarah felt as though she had been in heaven for a week, and now she was going back to hell.

What scared her most was what the speaker was saying about that mayonnaise jar. That slop in the jar was a snapshot of how Sarah felt about herself. She had stopped being happy when her mom and dad had divorced almost three years ago. Everybody had told her it would work out and that she would get used to it. But she never did. She just felt sad, really sad most of the time. When people tried to get her to have fun, she would catch herself laughing and know that it was fake. Her being such a downer had driven most of her friends away. Sarah was tempted to try drugs or beer, but that crowd was definitely not her type. Most of the time she spent alone at home, watching TV or listening to music—negative, angry music.

The worst experience of her life had started when her mom brought a boyfriend home. They were talking about getting married. Sarah wanted a man around if it would make her mom happy, but that all blew up. This guy was always around after school before Sarah's mother got home from work. Sarah has blocked out the details of what happened, but basically this guy would touch her and one day forced himself on her. It took Sarah three months to tell her mother what happened. She felt so dirty.

Of course the guy denied it. Sarah was shocked by her mom's initial reaction. She asked Sarah if she was lying about this just because she didn't want her mom to get married. That really hurt.

It was like a knife to the heart. Eventually her mom found out it was true and threw the guy out of the house, but that didn't repair the damage that had been done. Now her mom is unhappy all the time and drinks more than ever to deal with it. Every time Sarah thought about all those events in her life she went numb. *This is what I'm going home to. . . .*

Although the camp speaker was still talking, Sarah's mind was miles away as she considered how her life would change when the buses arrived. Her attention snapped back when the speaker pulled out a big white sheet. This was no camp cabin bunk sheet. It looked silky and expensive.

He threw the sheet over the mayo jar and the murky liquid. He made sure the jar was covered completely and said, "This is how God sees you when you put your faith in Christ—like so many of you did this week. What Jesus did by dying on the cross paid for our sins. When we put our trust in Him, God declares us 'not guilty,' and sees Jesus standing in our place. We still have a lot of the trash in our lives (like what's in this jar), but Jesus Christ and His blood cover us (like the sheet over the jar). In God's sight we are perfect and clean."

Those words gripped Sarah again, just as they had when she had heard them earlier in the week. The idea that God would love her and send Jesus to die for her was the best news she had ever heard. *Too good to be true*, she thought, until her counselor took a walk with her and explained how Christ had changed her life. Then she invited Sarah to receive Jesus and His forgiveness. That moment was unlike anything she had ever experienced. But now she was going home—back to reality. Ugh.

**How did you feel when someone first explained
Christ's love and forgiveness to you?**

How did you respond?

That reality seemed a million miles away from camp. All that had happened to her—the divorce, her sadness and depression, her isolation, the sexual abuse, the tension with her mother, and the distance that was growing between them as she watched her mother descend into more unhappiness and bitterness—had formed a huge pile of guilt and blame inside her. The junk in that mayonnaise jar wasn't nearly as bad as what she was made of.

How would that sheet over the jar help her when she was home? She had prayed and asked God to forgive her two days ago, but would she still be convinced she was forgiven and totally accepted by God after being home for a few weeks? It was good news that God loved her no matter what she did, but Sarah had to be realistic. Her life was a mess. How much of that would ever change?

Maybe this week was like what Sarah's mom had often said about "going on a cruise." Sure it was great to feel like royalty, eat all the fancy food, and see the sights, but when the week was over you had to come back home to regular life. Then all you had was less money and your tired memories of being happy for one week out of your life. Was this week at camp her cruise—one week of feeling good and then back to the messed-up, unhappy girl she really was?

Sarah knew that something deeper was happening inside her. The night before, some of the kids had made promises that they were going to stop specific bad activities when they got home. It was as though they had a couple of bad habits that with a little determination and self-control they could overcome and move on with their good lives. Sarah began to see that what was in her jar was much more tied to who she was and what she thought about herself.

The camp speaker switched gears and began talking about where Sarah's mind had been wandering—the challenge of going home. He took the sheet off the jar, revealing again the filthy water inside. Sarah guessed that the speaker would say that God loves us even though we will always be messed up. That counts for something if God can do that for us. All she has to do is get through seventy years of feeling bad by telling herself that God forgives her sins and will let her into heaven when she dies.

Sarah was wrong. The words out of the speaker's mouth were totally unexpected: "God not only wants to save us, He also wants to change us and transform us to become like Jesus Christ in the way we think and act." He pointed at the mayonnaise jar and asked the audience for ideas on how to get the water clear and clean again. "No, we can't pour it out and start over," he said. "We have to deal with what is real right now and still see if Jesus in us can change it for the better." He scanned the crowd, looking for a raised hand of someone with an idea, a suggestion, anything. Sarah shook her head. She didn't have a clue.

QUESTIONS TO PONDER
What is your solution? How can the camp speaker get the water clean?

SHAME RUNS DEEP

Sarah's story takes us to a deeper, darker reality than blame and condemnation. *Shame.* Our parents get mad and yell at us when we don't wash the dishes or clean our room. Sometimes they can get so upset that they may call us slobs or tell us we're lazy. Most of the time we feel bad about not doing what they asked us to do, and their yelling gets us to do what they want.

But shame is deeper and stronger than guilt. Shame is the belief that we did something wrong (or didn't do something right), so *we are not good people*. We personalize the blame and think that something is wrong with us—and we feel terrible. That's shame.

Shame runs deep. It involves more than just our reaction to our mistakes. It is an overriding feeling that we are worthless and rejected. We explain our mistakes by believing that those kinds of actions should be expected from someone who is as big a failure as we are. Shame destroys us inside. We expect the worst from ourselves because we believe that's who we really are. We're not surprised when we disappoint people because deep down inside we know we're no good.

Shame tells us, "I am what I am. I cannot change. I am hopeless." We think it can't be fixed. That is the way we are. Nothing works. Just live with it.

People who feel shame do different things to cope with how they feel. They deny it; they cover it up; they accept it and endure it. Shame attacks our spirit so severely that it makes us feel we are not good enough to be accepted.

In what way has your family most influenced how you see yourself?

Here is one final test to help you identify false beliefs in your life that are influencing how you see yourself and others. Continue to be honest as you answer these questions.

///

POP QUIZ

Write the correct number code in the blank next to each statement.

1 = Always
2 = Very Often
3 = Often
4 = Sometimes
5 = Seldom
6 = Very Seldom
7 = Never

_____ 1. I often think about past failures or experiences of rejection.

_____ 2. There are certain things about my past that I cannot recall without experiencing strong, painful emotions such as guilt, shame, anger, or fear.

_____ 3. I seem to make the same mistakes over and over again.

_____ 4. There are certain things about myself that I want to change, but I don't think it will ever happen.

_____ 5. I feel inferior to my friends.

_____ 6. There are aspects of my physical appearance that I hate.

_____ 7. I am generally disgusted with myself.

_____ 8. I feel that certain experiences have basically ruined my life.

_____ 9. I think of myself as a bad person who has broken many of God's rules.

_____ 10. I feel that I have lost the opportunity to experience a complete and wonderful life.

_____ **TOTAL**

Interpreting the Results

If your score was:

55–70: Congratulations! You have a strong appreciation for God's love and unconditional acceptance. You seem to be free from the feelings of shame that grip many people. Shame rarely influences your responses and approach to life. It may be only certain situations where feelings of shame control your responses to people.

30–54: You have moderate to strong feelings of shame. When you have emotional problems, they may relate to a sense of shame. If you reflect on your experiences, you may find that many of your previous decisions were related to your feelings of worthlessness. Many of your future decisions will also be affected by feelings of low self-esteem unless you take action to overcome these feelings of shame.

0–29: Shame has been a constant presence in your life. You feel its effects in your life almost every day. This robs you of the joy and peace that God wants to give you. Experiences of shame dominate your memory and have produced a good amount of depression and low self-esteem. These feelings will continue to dominate you until you experience a deep healing in your self-concept based on God's forgiveness and unconditional love.

If you ended up with a score that is lower than you'd prefer, don't panic. The rest of this chapter will guide you through God's awesome solution for freeing people from the feelings of shame.

THE SOURCES OF SHAME

Where does this shame come from? It comes from our own minds when we believe the negative messages from significant people in our lives. This feeling of being not wanted often begins at home, with the family.

Family Neglect.

Many teens grow up in families where the parent is too preoccupied to give them the attention and love they need. Some parents are so busy achieving success outside the home that their children don't get extended time with them. Instead, they get brief, scheduled minutes late at night or between activities on the weekends.

In other families the neglect stems from lack of attention because the parent is wrapped up in his or her own problems—depression, alcohol, or drugs. Parents with these struggles can't be counted on by their kids. In both situations, the kids get the message: "Raise yourself; we don't have time for you."

Before you start saying, "I wish my parents would just get off my back. What you described is exactly the kind of parents I want," remember that time is the best way to show a person you care about him or her. In our minds, "No time = No care. No care = No value." When parents seem to ignore their children, the children begin to think that they are not important enough to deserve their parents' time and attention.

Family Control.

On the other extreme are parents who dominate their kids' lives and rule their homes with authoritarian, iron fists. Parents like this assume that they know what is best for the child always and impose their views on just about everything related to their kids, now and in the future.

This approach makes you feel as though your life is not your own and that you cannot do anything to make your parents happy. Your self-worth becomes based entirely on your parents' desires and demands. You assume that something must be wrong with you if Mom or Dad don't think you are capable of making any decisions on your own.

Family Abuse.
The deepest shame comes from aggressive, attacking families. Verbal abuse, physical abuse, and sexual abuse often start when children are very young. The kids have no idea that what goes on in their homes is not "normal."

Verbal abuse includes sarcastic put-downs and ridicule that intimidates children into doing what parents want. Physical abuse involves hitting, withholding meals, or insisting on demeaning labor. It is done to make sure the kids know who is the boss. Sexual abuse strikes the deepest wound into young people's ideas of who they are. It invades the body of a child and creates a terrified young person, who is threatened by the abuser to keep "the secret" from the other significant people in the family circle. This type of abuse scars young people deeply and imprints shame in them.

HOW SHAME DESTROYS PEOPLE

Shame can have powerful effects on our self-worth. It shows up in how we live and what we do. Here are some of the results of shame:

Inferiority.

Shame breeds a deep sense of inferiority, the feeling that the person is not as good as everyone else. It may even cause someone to think they're a total loser, not worth anything at all. The feeling may come from numerous failure experiences or from a few memorable moments that knocked the person down.

Self-Destructive Behavior.

Your actions usually flow from your perception of yourself. If you see yourself through the eyes of shame, you'll develop a pessimistic outlook on life, and you could engage in self-destructive behaviors such as eating disorders (including compulsive eating), drug use, alcohol abuse, and reckless living.

Self-Pity.

Shame makes people see themselves as victims. They blame others or condemn themselves for their actions. They will sink into the depths of feeling sorry for themselves.

Withdrawal and Isolation.

Shame tells us to refuse taking chances in relationships or responsibilities. We know we will fail, so why try? We find time-consuming solo activities that keep us too busy to interact with others, adding to our loneliness.

Despising Appearance.

People don't have to be ugly to be ashamed of their appearance. Feeling ugly comes from what a person thinks he or she looks like compared to the standards of beauty in that person's mind.

Codependent Relationships.

In an attempt to overcome shame, a person can become addicted to the feeling of being needed by a family member or friend who has a problem or compulsion. Such a relationship can provide a sense of significance, but it often becomes a tool of manipulation against the shamed person.

WHOSE VOICE DO YOU BELIEVE?

Sarah feels the shame. She knows the sources of shame in her life. Her self-image is built on the evaluation of her behavior over the past sixteen years. Her memory is loaded with negatives: her par-

What experiences have brought you feelings of shame?

ents' divorce, the move to a new school, her extended time of sadness and depression, the rejection by friends, the lack of attention from her mother, the sexual abuse, her mother's reluctance to believe her, her mom's unhappiness being alone without a man. Day by day, Sarah builds her personality and self-worth on the "facts" of all these disappointments so far in her life.

Blame means "hearing the voices of others telling you that you don't meet the standards required to be cool or part of the crowd." *Shame* is hearing your own voice telling you that you are a failure for life and that you will never change.

The question is simple: Whom do you listen to? That is the main theme of this whole book. Each chapter has made the case that Satan tells us huge lies and that God responds with the truth. Who we listen to and how we react make the difference in whether our lives are filled with paralyzing negatives or liberating positives.

Take a look at several of Satan's lies below, and then read how God responds. Whom do you believe? Write out your response, that is, what you believe is true.

Satan says: "Your life is a mistake. It has no purpose or meaning."
God says: "God has made us what we are. In Christ Jesus, God
    made us to do good works, which God planned in advance
    for us to live our lives doing."[1]
You say: "I think the purpose of my life is _____

_____

_____

_____

Satan says: "You've done so many bad things that God will never accept you or forgive you."

God says: "So now, those who are in Christ Jesus are not judged guilty."[2]

You say: "With everything I have done, I think God will ____

_____

_____

_____

Satan says: "You will never change. What you are is what you always will be."

God says: "If anyone belongs to Christ, there is a new creation. The old things have gone; everything is made new!"[3]

You say: "I think the possibility of my life being changed is ___

_____

_____

_____

WE HAVE A CHOICE

The Bible says that we have a choice. We can break free from the negative forces in our pasts and be set free to live with new attitudes because of God's presence in our lives, or we can stay stuck in our pride and sinfulness. Paul said this is like getting rid of the old person and "becoming" a new person:

You were taught to leave your old self—to stop living the evil way you lived before. That old self becomes worse, because people are fooled by the evil things they want to do. But you were taught to be made new in your hearts, to become a new person. That new person is made to be like God—made to be truly good and holy.[4]

Ten key words (one phrase) in that verse identify what makes this change happen. Can you pick them out? While you are looking, remember that the shame young people feel is not some ink stamp on the back of a hand that washes off in a couple of days. Sarah and others who are tied up in shame would tell us that they wish it were as easy as "leaving your old self" and "becoming a new person," as though we are changing clothes to go to a special event. It's not that simple. This nasty stuff has been driven down deep into people.

Only one way exists to get this imprint changed from negative to positive, to move from the corrupted "old self" to the

What truths from God's Word have you poured into your heart recently?

"new self," which is in the likeness of God. Did you find the phrase? Take a pen and circle these ten words: "you were taught to be made new in your hearts." Or, as another version says: "You were taught to be renewed in the spirit of your mind" (NKJV).

The key to change is what we put into our hearts and minds. We sort through all the messages that come through our ears into our brains. We focus on certain messages and replay them constantly inside our heads. Those messages that get our full attention take root in us. From those messages that stick in our brains, we decide what we believe about ourselves, the world, and God. Our actions and behavior are the direct result of what we believe to be true. That explains why Satan works so hard to plant his lies into our minds and why God gives us His Word and tells us to read and think about it every day.

MAKING THE WATER CLEAN

The camp speaker had stumped the crowd. They had no answer for how to clean the polluted water in the mayonnaise jar. The speaker gave a paper cup to Josh, a young man in the front row, and asked him to fill it with water from the cooler at the back of the room. When Josh returned, the speaker told him to pour the clean water into the mayonnaise jar.

"Can you see the difference that one cup of clean water made in our jar?" the speaker asked. Everyone laughed. "Go get another cup of water," the speaker challenged Josh. Five times he sent him back to the water cooler. Each time, Josh poured the water into the jar with no apparent effect on the color or content of the liquid inside.

"Josh, do you believe that if you poured enough cups of water in the jar, we could make the water clear again?" the speaker asked.

With a sheepish look on his face, Josh shook his head no and said, "It sure doesn't look like it's making any difference."

The speaker put his arm around Josh's shoulder and turned to speak to the whole camp.

Pointing to the jar of water, he said, "This is your life. You had a lot of pollution and ugly stuff inside when you came to camp a week ago. During the week you heard the truth about it and the fact that God still loves you even with your polluted mind and life. He sent His own Son, Jesus Christ, into this world we live in and allowed Him to be crucified on a cross. When Jesus hung on that cross, God poured into His perfect, clean Son all the sin and pollution of the world so that we could be forgiven and justified (put right in God's sight). Today we dramatized that point by putting the sheet over the jar filled with the dirty water. God doesn't see our sin. He sees us covered by Jesus and His blood. We are completely forgiven. Now how are you going to take this home?"

Sarah leaned forward, listening intently. She would never get tired of hearing about God's love and forgiveness, but she was afraid of going home and losing everything she had learned at camp.

The speaker recruited fifteen kids off the floor to join Josh in the water brigade. He gave them each a cup and put them to work. As he spoke they carried cups of water to the jar and poured them in. "God accepts and forgives you as you are, but He wants to change your life by the renewing of your mind," the speaker continued. "The way He gets the old self out of you and builds a new self in you so that you will be like Jesus with righteousness and holiness is to pour His Word into you so that you will start to think like God. You will begin to see yourself as God sees you and begin to yield to God's way and obey Him in your daily actions and choices."

By this time the water being poured cup after cup into the mayonnaise jar was changing the color of the water. It was becoming lighter and clearer, and dirty water was spilling over the edges onto the floor. "What is happening in the jar is called displacement," explained the speaker. "When water is poured into a container, it pushes out the substance that was already there. The same thing is true about your mind and spirit. Satan has poured a lot of lies into your life. You think you are worthless, unlovable, and that you can never change. But just like the water in this jar is changing (and most of you thought that would be impossible), your mind can be changed and renewed when it is filled with the truth of God."

The speaker looked intently at the students. Sarah thought he was speaking directly to her.

"You and I will never be perfect," he said, "until we see Jesus face-to-face in heaven, but God wants to make you a new person and break the power of sin in your life. He wants to be in your life every day, changing the way you think, the way you talk, and how you live.

"Every day of your life He wants you to read His Word and pray and obey Him. When you do that, you will be pouring clear, clean living water into your polluted mind. God will make you a new person and destroy Satan's lie that says you cannot change."

In what part of your life do you need to push out the lies and pour in the truth?

TAKING IT HOME

Later, as Sarah walked toward the buses she prayed, "God, pour Your Word and truth into me. Help me to go home and be a light of hope for my mom. Renew my mind with Your truth. Every day show me my old destructive ways and teach me how to live a new life and be like Jesus."

Paul wrote to Titus about the same transformation process that Sarah prayed to experience:

> In the past we also were foolish. We did not obey, we were wrong, and we were slaves to many things our bodies wanted and enjoyed. We spent our lives doing evil and being jealous. People hated us, and we hated each other. But when the kindness and love of God our Savior was shown, he saved us because of his mercy. It was not because of good deeds we did to be right with him. He saved us through the washing that made us new people through the Holy Spirit. God poured out richly upon us that Holy Spirit through Jesus Christ our Savior. Being made right with God by his grace, we could have the hope of receiving the life that never ends.[5]

Shame grips us and tells us we are no good, that we will never change. God tells us we are so valuable that He would sacrifice the life of His only Son, Jesus, to provide all we need in order to be reconciled to Him. God wants to make us part of His family, to give us new life and a new way of thinking about who we are and our purpose in life.

God wants to pour His truth into us every day. The first few deposits of truth may not seem to make much difference, but the day-by-day pouring will bring the change God promises. It's a lifetime process to push out the lies and displace them with God's truth. Don't give in to the shame that Satan is trying to tattoo on you. God wants to set you free.

RECAP

Shame is a deep-rooted personal belief that the mistakes we make are evidence that we are worthless failures who can never change. We learn this message in our families and from significant people in our lives. This shame produces destructive and pessimistic attitudes in us and sentences us to a life of failure. God not only forgives us for all our sins when we confess them, but He also regenerates us by the work of the Holy Spirit and the renewing of our minds. The renewing process is a long, steady commitment to putting God's truth into our minds and pushing out the lies of Satan.

Pour God's Word into your mind this week by:

⇒ Reading and studying the following passages that describe the stable, secure identity we have in Christ. It is our privilege to be His children, to experience His love, forgiveness, and power, and then to express to others how much we love Him.

⇒ Responding by writing in your own words what these passages say about the relationship God wants to have with you:

Passage	What God Is Telling You About Your New Life in Him
Matthew 5:13–14	
Romans 5:17–18	
Romans 8:1–17	
2 Corinthians 5:17–21	
Galatians 2:20	
Ephesians 2:4–10	
Colossians 3:12	
1 Peter 1:16	
1 John 4:17	

VERSES TO READ

1. Ephesians 2:10
2. Romans 8:1
3. 2 Corinthians 5:17
4. Ephesians 4:22-24
5. Titus 3:3-7

6

THE BIG LIES

"WHO WILL I BELIEVE?"

Believe a big lie—pay a big price. It's always been true. That's why we've spent so many pages identifying and exposing the big lies of Satan. Believe them and they will destroy your life.

Eric bought the big lie. He started giving his parents real trouble about church and youth group when he was fourteen. They fought hard for a year. His parents got tired—actually they started fighting with each other about what Eric was doing. They gave up. Eric hasn't been to church (except for holidays) for two years. The youth leader used to call him every month to be friendly and invite him to events, but now he has given up, too.

These days Eric spends his weekends doing the fast party scene. He runs with a crowd that lives on the edge of reckless. Drinking is their specialty. They party at friends' houses when their parents are gone and go through cases of beer most weekends. The drinking has accelerated to new levels during the winter of this senior year. They start earlier, get drunk quicker, and stay hung over all weekend.

Eric thinks the freedom is great. His parents have turned their heads and stopped trying to interfere with his life. Only his thirteen-year-old sister has the guts to talk straight with him. She hears the stories from her school friends. This week she laid into Eric about wasting his life. He wanted to smack her, but you can't be mad at your kid sister—especially when she is right. He knows that his life is going nowhere. He and his friends do the same thing every Friday and Saturday night. It sounds crazy to admit it, but all this so-called wild living is becoming so predictable. Every time they try something new, it gets old in a hurry. Eric feels bored and scared sometimes about what his life is becoming.

From what you have seen, what makes someone drop out of church and start believing Satan's lies?

THE LIES WE BELIEVE

The lie that pulled Eric away from church and his parents is an old, familiar one. It goes like this: "God is antifun." So if God is against getting drunk, getting drunk must be fun. You can either have a wild, exciting life stiff-arming God or a dull, boring one doing the go-to-church-God-thing. Take your pick. Eric made his choice, and now he is living with the consequences.

Sin is so overrated. The television commercials work—they're very effective. Marketing gurus know we are hungry for relationships and fun. Check out the beer adverts. Most use humor to soften us up and feature young adults in cool places having fun together. They also, almost always, highlight sex. And we buy it. The rest of the story (what happens after the drinking) never gets told. The same is true for gambling, smoking, drugs, pornography, sex, and the whole list. After a while, it's all boring.

While working in the kitchen at a youth retreat, one of the college-age dishwashers picked up a funnel (if you don't know what one is, go ask your mom) and started laughing. He held the funnel up to his eye like a telescope and said, "Looking through this is like looking at life. If you look through the wide end, you see a narrow, restricted view of life on the other side. Jesus said that many people walk on a wide road that leads them to destruction.[1] The wide side of the funnel says anything goes—try it all, but it leads to a restricted, narrow life. Just ask any alcoholic or drug addict. Watch what happens to families when parents cheat on each other. The results always bring less freedom and more sadness."

But then he turned the funnel around and looked through the bottom, narrow hole. He said, "When you look this direction, the view starts small but opens up to a wider and wider view the farther you go." He continued, "Jesus finished His story by saying there was also a narrow road that leads to life, but few people find it.[2] When you live for Christ, you walk into the rest of your life without addictions, STDs, guilt, and bad memories. Yes, there are some restrictions that make you act and talk different from most other people your age, but those restrictions protect you from the destructive results of Satan's lies. God opens doors for future opportunities you never dreamed possible!"

CHOOSING THE NARROW ROAD

Trent used to be tight with Eric when they were younger. When Eric started busting loose from his parents and church, Trent was tempted to join him, but he was more cautious and thoughtful about the trouble that comes with rebellion and unrestrained freedom. Instead, Trent got more involved in the youth ministry of the church. He heard some nasty comments from Eric and other kids at school about being wimpy. It was hard to be different from the guys who were his friends, but he chose that narrow path and stuck to it.

Today Trent has several years of evidence that God didn't ruin his life. In truth, his life has been filled with more excitement and adventure than he could have ever predicted.

He has been on two summer mission trips, one to Appalachia and one to Honduras. His group helped build and repair houses for two weeks. Trent learned how to roof a house. His whole perspective of the world and life changed after spending time with people who have little money yet are so happy. Working with Christians on these projects has given Trent a different view of what he wants his life to be. According to Trent, "God's people rock because they get involved and give what they have to help improve bad situations rather than sit back with a negative, 'whatever' attitude."

Trent will say that God hasn't cheated him out of any fun either. The youth group meetings on Friday nights are crazy. But this is crazy stuff without any negative consequences. Life isn't any easier for Trent than it is for his distant friend Eric, but Trent has a positive hope about whatever comes into his life. He has learned that God is real and that God cares about people and answers prayers. Life is exciting when God is involved and we are connected to Him.

Eric and Trent share similar backgrounds. They both were brought up in the church by good parents. They both heard the lies of Satan and the false beliefs that dominate this world. Trent rejected those lies and Eric embraced them (at least, so far). Trent embraced God and His response to the lies. Eric isn't paying attention to God right now. Their lives are headed in different directions because of choices they made.

> What decisions have you made about your life during the past year? Has reading this book caused you to change any of your decisions? What course are you setting for your future?

BEATING BACK THE BIG LIES SURVEY

Read this summary of the four big lies that have messed up the way we think about life and how we see ourselves. After each one, write your response in the space provided.

Big Lie #1: "I must meet certain standards to feel good about myself."

Believing this lie produces:

⇒ A strong fear of failure

⇒ A desire to do everything perfectly

⇒ An inner drive to succeed and to be valued and loved

⇒ A willingness to manipulate others to achieve my own success

⇒ Frequent withdrawing from challenging opportunities because of fear of failure

Your response: In what ways do you feel the pressure to achieve so that you will feel good about yourself? Which of these results listed above do you see in your life now?

God's truth about you: God loves you fully because of who you are, not what you do. Nothing you do makes God love you more. None of your failures make God love you less. You are not guilty in God's eyes because Christ died for you on the cross. This has nothing to do with what you have done for God or whether you deserve it. Your life is valuable because of the price God paid to set you free. You are completely forgiven and fully pleasing to God. You no longer have to fear failure.

Believing the truth produces:

⇒ Increasing freedom from the fear of failure

⇒ Confidence that my life is significant and valuable

⇒ Freedom to try new experiences and challenges

⇒ Desire to pursue Jesus Christ and everything He wants me to do

⇒ Great love for Christ and thankfulness for what He has done for me

Your response: How does God's forgiveness affect how you feel about yourself and the purpose of your life? _____

_____

_____

_____

Big Lie #2: "I must be approved and accepted by certain people in my life to feel good about myself."

Believing this lie produces:

⇒ A strong fear of rejection

⇒ Attempting to please others and fit in at any cost

⇒ Being overly sensitive to criticism

⇒ Withdrawing and spending most time alone to avoid possible disapproval by others

⇒ Being fearful of what people say about me

Your response: Describe how much what other people think about you influences what you do. _____

_____

_____

_____

God's truth about you: You are totally and completely accepted by God because of what Jesus Christ did for you. In God's sight you are His child. He will never let anything separate you from His love. You are accepted by God and no longer have to fear rejection from people.

Believing the Truth produces:

⇒ Increasing freedom from the fear of rejection

⇒ Willingness to be open and vulnerable

⇒ Ability to relax around others

⇒ Willingness to take criticism

⇒ Desire to please God no matter what others think

Your response: How does knowing that God completely accepts you help you deal with what other people think of you?

_____

_____

_____

Big Lie #3: "Those who fail (including me) are unworthy of love and deserve to be punished."

Believing this lie produces:

⇒ Feelings of guilt about most things I do

⇒ Fear of punishment

⇒ Tendency to punish others the way I punish myself

⇒ Blaming myself and others for any personal failures

⇒ Withdrawing from God and friends because I don't feel worthy

⇒ Feeling driven to do anything I can to avoid punishment

Your response: How does the way I treat other people tell the story about how I feel about myself? _____

_____

_____

_____

God's truth about you: Jesus paid the full price for your sin. You don't have to feel guilty, because what Jesus did for you settled your debt with God completely. You are deeply loved by God. You no longer have to fear punishment or punish others for your failures.

Believing the truth produces:

⇒ Less guilt about failures and shortcomings

⇒ Increasing freedom from the fear of punishment

⇒ Patience and kindness toward others

⇒ Learning to accept forgiveness from God and others

⇒ A deep love for Christ and growing love for others

Your response: What guilt do you feel that is hard to release? Whom have you been able to forgive in the same way that God has forgiven you? _____

_____

_____

_____

Big Lie #4: "I am what I am. I cannot change. I am hopeless."
Believing this lie produces:

⇒ Feelings of shame, hopelessness, inferiority, passivity

⇒ Isolation

⇒ Withdrawal from others

Your response: What do you dislike about yourself that seems so difficult to change? _____

_____

_____

_____

God's truth about you: You have been made brand-new and complete in Christ. You no longer need to experience the pain of shame. You can change through the power of the Holy Spirit working in you. God's word and promises will replace the lies in your mind that have held you back from being the person you were created to be.

Believing the truth produces:

⇒ A Christ-centered self-confidence

⇒ A new joy

⇒ Courage to make changes in your life

⇒ Peace of mind and heart

⇒ A growing desire to know Christ

Your response: What important changes has Christ made in your life? What additional changes would you like to see Christ make in your life in the future? _____

_____

_____

_____

If you have been identifying these four big lies of Satan and dealing with how they have influenced your life, you are on your way toward freedom. Knowing God's truth and applying it to your feelings of inferiority, condemnation, and blame can radically change how you feel about yourself and your life. Enjoy the freedom and acceptance that Jesus purchased for you on the cross.

Dealing with these lies and removing them from controlling our lives is a lifelong commitment. Don't be afraid of this. God's truth makes Satan run. His destructive ideas look foolish when we put them next to God's words and actions for us. God makes a commitment to us when we put our faith and trust in Christ. He will keep His promises to us and never leave us alone to fight our enemy. But don't think Satan will disappear and give up trying to confuse us by twisting God's truth. He is always trying to undermine our trust in God and our focus on His truth, especially about who we are.

CAN YOU TRUST GOD WITH YOUR LIFE?

This is a big question for everyone, especially when you are young. Eric and Trent came up with totally different answers. Despite all the evidence we have from God's Word and from watching the lives of people who know God, we still have our doubts. Jesus' disciples had the same question. Peter asked Jesus, "Look, we have left everything and followed you. So what will we have?"[3]

The writer of Psalm 73 looked around and saw that the people who were ignoring God were having more fun than he was following God. Life looked easy for the wicked and hard for him, the God-seeker. How is that fair? He was so upset by what he was seeing that he almost changed his mind to join the wicked; but something stopped him. God showed him the ultimate destiny of people who ignore and disobey Him: "It was too hard for me to see until I went to the Temple of God. Then I understood what will happen to them. You have put them in danger; you cause them to be destroyed."[4] God's message to the person questioning the reward of following God is: Look down the road and see where you are headed and where the wicked are headed. Remember what Jesus said, "The wide road leads to destruction; the narrow road leads to life."

GOD FORGIVES ME, BUT MY LIFE IS STILL A MESS

"It is finished!" Jesus cried out from the cross.[5] The greatest moment in history had arrived. Jesus fulfilled the mission and purpose of God. Our redemption was complete. The price had been paid so that our sins could be forgiven and our reconciliation with God could become a reality. Nothing more needs to be done to win God's favor. All that remains for us to do is respond to God as we hear His Word. He wants us to believe and put our hope and trust in Jesus Christ as our Lord and Savior.

When we give our lives to Christ, it's as though God bought our house. As the new owner, He starts a major renovation and fix-up project on the house (that's us). Maybe we have a hole in the roof or bad plumbing. He accepts us as we are and starts the cleanup and repair. It doesn't happen overnight—it will last a lifetime. Regardless of the shape we are in, He promises to see His project through to completion. Here's how Paul describes the commitment that God has to us: "God began doing a good work in you, and I am sure he will continue it until it is finished when Jesus Christ comes again."[6]

If your life were a house that God is renovating, what fix-up or remodeling projects would God put on the list for immediate work to make you more like Jesus?

God (the new owner of our house) brings all the materials and tools needed to get the job done. He wants to get the lies of Satan out of our minds, just like a builder wants to clean out the termites and toxic waste from the basement so the foundation will be solid and the space will be a healthy place to live. God wants to rebuild our house (and our lives) one day at a time, repairing the leaks and holes caused by years of neglect and abuse by the previous owner. The process is tiring and slow. Some days we become discouraged and ready to quit. We reach a point where we can live with what changes He has made so far. We get comfortable and wonder why more needs to be done. But God (the builder of strong lives) keeps rolling out the blueprints and building plans (when we read His Word) to remind us how great the finished house will be. He has much bigger dreams for us than we can imagine.

When we need motivation, we remember how much He paid for our house (when Jesus died on the cross), so we can keep working with Him on the renovation and remodeling. The apostle Peter lays out God's work plan for how He wants to remodel us by building these strong character qualities in us layer by layer:

> Because you have these blessings, do your best to add these things to your lives: to your faith, add goodness; and to your goodness, add knowledge; and to your knowledge, add self-control; and to your self-control, add patience; and to your patience, add service for God; and to your service for God, add kindness for your brothers and sisters in Christ; and to this kindness, add love. If all these things are in you and are growing, they will help you to be useful and productive in your knowledge of our Lord Jesus Christ. But anyone who does not have these things cannot see clearly. He is blind and has forgotten that he was made clean from his past sins.[7]

That's a lot of renovation work God wants to do on us. He wants to make us like Jesus Christ. That means the same personal character qualities Jesus showed when He lived here on earth are the ones God wants to install and develop in us. That's a huge plan that can seem impossible, but He knows what's best for us and He won't give up. He paid plenty for us. We are valuable to Him.

Don't get discouraged. All this happens one day at a time. Life is never predictable, but in all the surprises God keeps His promise to be with us. He doesn't let us go through more than we can handle (with His help). Just as we trusted Christ to save us, so now we can trust Him with each day's problems. If we listen, He gives us the help we need for our decisions and choices, right up to the day when our life on earth is over and we go to heaven. When we cross into that new life, God's renovation plans for us will be finished perfectly. We will be exactly who He created us to be.

WE CAN'T DO THIS—SEND A HELPER

If all this "house renovation" that still needs to be done makes you tired just thinking about it, don't worry. We don't have to do it all by ourselves! God sends us a Helper—the Holy Spirit.

When Jesus told His disciples everything He wanted them to do, they almost panicked. They were struggling to get it done when Jesus was with them. How could they do it alone after He had left them? Jesus assured them that they would not be doing it alone. "I will ask the Father, and he will give you another Helper to be with you forever."[8]

Jesus' promise was fulfilled just fifty days later (after Jesus had returned to heaven) when the Holy Spirit came to empower and direct the believers at Pentecost. The same Holy Spirit lives in all people who are believers in Jesus Christ today. He serves as our Teacher, Counselor, and source of spiritual Power as we live for Christ's glory and honor.

The Holy Spirit empowers believers. When the Bible uses the phrase "The Spirit of the Lord came upon him," it means that God gave a temporary and spontaneous increase of physical, spiritual, or mental strength to a person. This was a supernatural occurrence to prepare a person for a special task. When has God given you a special increase of strength for a special job He wanted you to do?

What do you know about the Holy Spirit? This is the third Person of the Trinity (the Father, the Son, and the Holy Spirit). The Holy Spirit is God and possesses all the characteristics of God. The primary purpose of the Holy Spirit is to glorify Christ.[9] The Holy Spirit is our Teacher so that we can understand the Bible.[10] It is by the Holy Spirit's power that the love of Christ flows through us and produces spiritual fruit within us. This fruit is the collection of changes that God makes in us when we obey Him. It includes intimate friendship with Christ,[11] love for each other,[12] joy and peace when life is difficult,[13] perseverance,[14] and the ability to bring others to Christ and help them become His disciples.[15] The fruit of the Holy Spirit is love, joy, peace, patience, kindness, goodness, faithfulness, gentleness, and self-control.[16]

God knows that we will struggle and have problems in this world because Satan is the ruler here (temporarily). He is actively trying to get us to believe his lies. God has not left us alone in this world. The Holy Spirit is present in us if we have asked Jesus Christ to be our Lord and Savior. He will give us strength, comfort, and guidance. Even on the worst days of our lives when we doubt that God could ever love or forgive us, the Holy Spirit is right beside us, reminding us that God loves and accepts us completely, no matter what happens.

NO FANATICS, PLEASE

Think about it—Jesus came to earth from *heaven*. He knows first-hand who God is—how good, powerful, forgiving, and holy God is. Jesus saw people face-to-face who couldn't even comprehend what God could produce in their lives because they were so distracted by trivial stuff that wouldn't last very long. Many of these folks were highly religious people. They didn't even come close to experiencing what God had planned for them because their contact with Him was so superficial. There are still people who wonder if God is really there or if He cares about what is happening here on earth.

So Jesus told His followers a story about a farmer who scattered seeds in his field. Jesus described what happened to the seeds when they landed on different types of ground.[17]

⇒ The first seeds landed on hard ground and were eaten by the birds.

⇒ The second seeds landed on rocky soil. They started to grow, but the roots couldn't get past the rocks. In the heat of the day, they wilted because they had no roots deep enough to draw up any moisture from the ground.

⇒ The third seeds landed in soil that was infested by weeds. As the seeds sprouted and grew, so did the weeds. The good plants got choked out by the weeds and died.

⇒ The fourth seeds landed in good soil, sprouted, and grew up
to produce fruit—lots of it.

On the surface, the story seems to say that farmers have to
work hard and be smart to get results from the seeds they plant.
The odds are against the seeds being able to do what they were
created to do—produce much good fruit (and more seeds).

At the end of the story, however, Jesus explained its meaning.
Jesus wanted to make sure that His disciples (and we) understood
that this story was about how people respond to God's Word. The
seed the farmer is sowing is God's Word.

The hard soil, where the first seeds landed and were quickly
eaten by the birds, represents people who never respond to God's
Word. It never gets inside their minds. They are hardened toward
God and don't get it.

The rocky soil, where the second seeds landed and quickly
wilted, represents people who receive God's Word and have a
brief experience with God, but they don't let the Word get very
deep in them. When trouble or persecution comes, they give up
quickly.

The weed-infested soil, where the third seeds landed and got
choked, represents the people who receive God's Word but don't
do much with it. They are busy making money, buying material
possessions, and worrying about being accepted by others more
than they are focused on making God most important in their life.
In the end, the hunt for money and comfortable living squeezes
out God's message.

The good soil, where the fourth seeds landed and grew, represents people who hear God's Word and accept it fully into their lives. The seeds grow and deliver a huge crop.

What competes with your commitment to Christ for first place in your life?

What has hindered your growth as a Christian? What weeds or rocky ground have you had in your life the past year?

So let's put ourselves right there beside Jesus and let Him speak to us. He looks us in the eye and says, "Be careful, young men and women. I have come to give you life, but an enemy prowls throughout this world who will do everything he can to keep you from getting connected with Me. If you want Me and My message in your life, you must make Me the top priority. Watch out when you go to church or to a Christian camp. Satan, your enemy, will let you say yes to Me as often as you want—as long as you don't get serious about Me. He will try to convince you that a shallow connection with Me is good enough. Then when the pressure is on, you will collapse because you won't have your life roots growing down into Me. He will say that being a Christian is fine, just don't become a fanatic about it. You can keep all the old habits and attitudes that are corrupting your life. Just go to church once a week and go through the motions. Everyone will think you are a great person, and you can spend the rest of your week doing whatever it takes to impress other people, be successful, and feel good."

Can you see Jesus' eyes looking lovingly and intently at you? He continues speaking quietly but with power, "I came to this earth to make it possible for you to have a personal relationship with God. Nothing is more important than knowing Me. If you want Me in your life, don't do it halfway. God wants to do a great and mighty work in you, but it means putting Me first above everything else. Get rid of the bad stuff, and put the good stuff in second place after Me. Get yourself ready for Me, and you will see results (fruit) like you have never imagined."

So what do you do now? Go back to watching TV?

God is calling you to a brand-new life and away from the old lies of this world.

What's your answer?

NO TIME FOR SELF-SABOTAGE

If you are struggling as a Christian and not experiencing God's presence and power, or if you are a new Christian who wants to avoid the stupid mistakes some Christians make, here are four ways *not* to shoot yourself in the foot (or worse) as a Christian.

No Stockpiling Sin.

As a Christian, you will continue to sin because you are a human being. Sin is when we ignore God and disobey what He tells us. God has made a way for us to deal with sin. We confess it and agree with God that it is not what we want or what is good for us. God forgives us and cleanses us. We move forward with our eyes wide open, trying to make the right choice the next time.

Stockpiling sin is willfully continuing to do what we know is wrong. We have developed some strong habits and desires that are hard to break. Don't beat yourself up with guilt. It may take some time to change the way you think about yourself and others as well as to change your actions. What you don't want to do is believe the lie that it doesn't matter to God since He forgives you anyway. God does forgive you, but doing what displeases Him hurts your relationship with Him. If temptation stays strong, ask other Christians to help you deal with it. Get into an accountability relationship and talk about what is happening in your life. Pray together and encourage each other to seek God's best.

Know to Grow.

There is so much to learn about God. What you have experienced so far as a new Christian is a tiny part of all that God wants to teach you about Himself, yourself, and your life together. God has given us the greatest resource—His Word, the Bible. Dig into this book, knowing that you are reading supernatural communication. Get into a good basic Bible study with a teacher/mentor at your church to guide you. Read your Bible every day. Fill your mind with the words of God, and God will give you endurance and hope to get through the tough situations of life.[18]

Don't let laziness or distractions keep you from growing in both knowledge and experience. Don't be like the grandmother whose grandchildren bought her a computer so they could send her e-mails and photos from across the country, but because she hadn't learned fully how to use her e-mail, all she did was play solitaire. She missed all that her grandchildren wanted to send her because she didn't learn how to use this new machine.

Learn all you can about the Holy Spirit (as we discussed earlier in this chapter). Don't overlook or underestimate the power available to you from the Holy Spirit to help you change your life and love others as Christ did. Study the fruit of the Holy Spirit[19] and ask God to help you develop these attitudes and actions in your life. Let the Holy Spirit reveal changes that God wants to make in you. You can be confident of God's steadfast love for you because of the presence of the Holy Spirit in your life.

Avoid the Extremes.

Two dimensions of the Christian life seem miles apart from each other: (1) human self-discipline and (2) dependence on supernatural or human feelings. A strong, growing Christian is always working on a balance of these two experiences.

We need the discipline of reading the Bible and praying on a regular schedule. That doesn't mean we only do it at the scheduled times. It's like eating. We eat when we get hungry, but we also have a normal three-meal-a-day schedule that keeps us healthy and well nourished. Discipline is a spiritual activity that is vital to Christian growth. The extreme to avoid is being so rigidly committed to the schedule of study, prayer, and service that we could miss something God wants us to do. The other danger is the pride and a performance-oriented attitude you may develop if your focus is only on completing the scheduled tasks. Our relationship with God is not built on what we do to please God but on His grace and mercy to us.

Both human and supernatural feelings are alive in the life of a Christian. The Holy Spirit guides and directs us in a new way beyond what we have known in the past. The challenge is to learn to discern what feelings are promptings of the Holy Spirit and what feelings are merely human emotions (perhaps even self-serving feelings). This is a lifelong learning experience. We don't have to wait for God to give us a motivating *feeling* to do what the Bible clearly says we should do. Feelings that go against what the Bible teaches are definitely not the "leading of the Holy Spirit." Our emotions are God-given; it is not wrong to have them. But feelings aren't reliable enough to determine God's direction.

Understanding God's leading requires that we blend a proper understanding of the Scriptures with sensitivity to His Holy Spirit. We also need to develop sensitivity to the Holy Spirit's leading that goes beyond feelings and emotions. This discernment takes time to develop and is based on three vital sources: (1) the clear teaching of the Scriptures, (2) previous experiences with the message of the Holy Spirit, and (3) the agreement of mature believers.

It's Him, Not It.

Sometimes we forget the basic reason why we are Christians. If coming to Christ has helped us get free of an addiction or get through a terrible tragedy, we can start thinking of being a Christian as merely a means to a desired end. When Holly became a Christian, she was recovering from a terrible breakup with her boyfriend. When he rejected her, she found acceptance in Christ. What happens to Holly when she gets a new boyfriend? Does Jesus still have the top place in her heart? Do we take Christ into our lives just to get through our problems or until our problems are solved?

Neil told his youth leader that he was dropping out of youth group because he just wasn't into it anymore. It just wasn't as real to him as it used to be. The youth leader was quiet for a while before responding. Finally he said, "Neil, I heard what you said— you're not into it anymore. My question for you is, who is *it?* Being a Christian isn't being in a program or a self-help group. It's not a seminar you are taking. Being a Christian is about a personal relationship that God wants to have with you through Jesus Christ. That's *Him,* not *it.* So what you are saying is that you're not into Him anymore and that He's not as real to you as He used to be."

God wants us to know Him and love Him. The meetings, the trips, and all the rest are great opportunities to get to learn about Him and be with other people who love Him, but involvement in these activities means little or nothing if we are not committed followers of Him—Jesus Christ.

IT'S YOUR CHOICE

The day Jesus told the story of the farmer and the seeds, Peter stood right there, hearing His voice and looking into His eyes. Years later, after much experience following Jesus, Peter wrote this challenge: "So prepare your minds for service and have self-control. All your hope should be for the gift of grace that will be yours when Jesus Christ is shown to you."[20]

"Prepare your minds for service."

Remember Trent? He is getting ready for a life filled with adventure, challenge, and excitement as he follows Jesus. Peter confirms that life following Jesus will be thrilling.

"Have self-control."

This isn't just about not overeating and staying sexually pure. Those are strong desires where we need God's help, but the biggest battle is in our heads. We control what gets repeated in our minds. Thoughts come in that we can't control. Some are true; many are lies. What we *can* control are the ideas that get repeated, what we think about over and over. Use your self-control to throw out the lies of Satan when they try to worm their way into your mind. Focus your thoughts on what God says about you and His love for you.

"All your hope should be for the gift of grace that will be yours when Jesus Christ is shown to you."

A great day is coming when what we are doing by faith right now will become completely real. Here on earth we have days when we wonder if God really does love us and forgive us. Peter says that the time is coming when we will hear it and see it in person; we will be face to face with Jesus. Believe His promise today and live that way right now. On that future day you will find out how right you have been.

Trent has put his life in God's control. Someday he will see that he wasn't a fool to fully believe God's Word.

Eric has missed it so far, but we are praying and hoping that he will wake up to God's love and forgiveness. We know that God hasn't given up on him.

How about you? Are you in? Are you ready to beat back the lies, believe God's truth, and put your life fully in God's control?

VERSES TO READ:

1. Matthew 7:13
2. Matthew 7:14

3. Matthew 19:27
4. Psalm 73:16–18
5. John 19:30
6. Philippians 1:6
7. 2 Peter 1:5–9
8. John 14:16
9. John 16:14
10. John 16:13
11. John 15:14
12. John 15:12
13. John 14:27
14. Romans 5:3–5
15. Matthew 28:18–20
16. Galatians 5:22–23
17. Matthew 13:1–23
18. Romans 15:4
19. Galatians 5:22–23
20. 1 Peter 1:13

7

MOTIVATION AND GUILT

"I SHOULD *BE GOOD*"

Matt stood outside the motel room watching Ryan smoke a cigarette. "I guess I don't look like a 'church boy' anymore, do I?" Ryan said boldly. "It's just not worth it—all the guilt they lay on you."

They were driving home from college and this was an unexpected overnight stop after the car had broken down. Matt, finishing his first semester, had grabbed a ride with Ryan and his friends, who were two years older. The car would be repaired by noon tomorrow, but tonight they were roommates at this cheap motel.

Matt and Ryan attended the same church at home. They didn't know each other well because of the two-year age difference, but everyone knew Ryan. His father was the pastor. That's what made the whole trip home a little uncomfortable for Matt. The language, the music, and the smoking seemed so drastically different from the

Ryan that Matt had seen in church when he was growing up. Matt thought he would see Ryan at the Christian Campus Fellowship group when he started at the college this fall. Now he was getting a clear picture of why Ryan had been nowhere near that group all semester.

"Want a smoke?" Ryan offered Matt the pack. Matt shook his head no. "Hey, they won't kill you, . . . or will they?" Ryan laughed as he stashed the pack in his jacket. "Well, you can go home and tell everybody that the old Ryan—Mr. Church Boy—is dead. He died at college and was born again as a guy who wanted to be free from God-guilt and have some good times in this life."

> **How have the expectations of other Christians put negative pressure on you?**

Matt stayed silent. He didn't know how to respond. What he saw in Ryan wasn't much different from most of the guys he had met during his first semester. It wasn't his place to judge Ryan, but the way Ryan had changed in two years from what he appeared to be in high school was huge. Matt took a risk and asked, "So Ryan, what turned you off of church and God?"

"It was lots of things," Ryan snapped back, "but there were a couple of big ones. I got a fresh start figuring out life at college and realized how much guilt my parents and all their church friends had piled on me. According to them, everything fun makes God mad. If I didn't act the way they expected, then God was going to get me. I got sick of living like that and bagged it.

"Now let me ask you a question," Ryan continued. "You look like the kind of kid my father would like to have for his son. You've been acting pretty holy on this trip home. You say no to all the things on the church's 'No-No List.' So here's the question—do you do all this good living because this is really what you *want* to do, or because people told you this is what you *should* do to be a good Christian and you are afraid to disappoint them and have them reject you?"

Matt hesitated. That was a tough question. He wanted to say it was because that's what he wanted to do, but the pressure to please other Christians was real, too. "I don't know," Matt said quietly. "A little of both, I guess."

"I can respect that," Ryan said looking away, "but can I tell you what really turned me off to the whole Christian thing? I watched what went on in the church and in my own family and decided that most of the time the people telling me what to do were trying to make me feel bad for just being human so they could get me to act the way *they* thought was holy and right. They had me feeling guilty about everything I did or said because it would hurt my parents or damage my father's reputation as a pastor. Did you care what I did? I don't think so. I couldn't live like that. It's sick. I'm not proud of everything I do now, but at least

I'm not making myself ill thinking about whether or not God will punish me for it. I don't think He cares—it is all the petty people in the church who act like God's police. From what I've seen, most of them have their own junk. They just cover it up."

Ryan flicked his cigarette into the parking lot. "Sorry, kid, didn't mean to mess you up," he said as he opened the door into the room and disappeared inside.

Matt wanted to respond, but this conversation was over. Maybe that was better. No way was he going to change Ryan's outlook on life. But Ryan's question was a good one. How much of what he did as a Christian was really what he wanted to do, and how much was to please others and show them he was a good Christian? He'd have to think about that.

GUILT WORKS

Guilt is an effective tool used to influence others to be the way we want them to be. It can be openly expressed with clear intentions to hurt, control, or punish. More often it is subtle and not meant to control or hurt. It just works—so we use it.

When have you heard parents say something like this to their kids?

> *If you really loved your father, you would do more around the house to help him out.*
>
> Translation: "You're lazy and we can't get you to work."

We feel so embarrassed when you go out dressed that way—like we are bad parents.

Translation: "You look ridiculous. We want you to dress the way we do."

Your behavior causes all kinds of arguments and tensions in this house. Why are you making it so hard on our whole family?

Translation: "Please shut up and go along with what we say."

Or when have you caught yourself saying to your parents something like this?

If you really trusted me, you would let me go with all my friends to the beach for the weekend.

Translation:

Everybody else gets to stay out until 2:00 A.M. Why did I get stuck in such a bad family?

Translation:

Or have you said to your friends something like this?

You can go out with those other people. Why would it make me feel bad to stay home alone on Friday night?

Translation:

Guilt works so well that some church leaders can't resist using it to get us to be better Christians. When you get God involved, the guilt really grabs us. Try this one: *How can you expect God to answer your prayers if you are not going to church regularly and reading your Bible every day?*

Analyze that statement. How is the fact that God answers prayer connected to going to church and reading the Bible? From all you have read in this book, what is wrong with motivating a person to come to church this way? It's based on performance, right? This statement suggests that getting God to care enough about us to answer our prayers requires that we must go to church and read our Bible. The guilt here is *false* guilt. To suggest that the reason our prayers aren't being answered is because of what we aren't doing puts all the blame back on us. That's just where Satan wants it.

How does guilt play either a positive or negative role in your life?

In contrast, *true* guilt comes from the condition of being separated from God and deserving condemnation for sin. We stand guilty before God. It is genuine guilt when we know in our hearts that we have ignored God and disobeyed His commandments. When we are gripped by these guilt feelings, which come from the presence of sin in us and from the Holy Spirit sending a You-Need-God signal to our hearts and minds, there is only one solution. We must turn to God and trust in the work of Jesus Christ and His death on the cross to be forgiven and cleansed from our sin.

In the New Testament, guilt has a restricted meaning. It refers only to people *before* they put their faith in Christ. Once we come to Christ and put our faith in Him and in what He did on the cross, we face no condemnation from God.

So now, those who are in Christ Jesus are not judged guilty. Through Christ Jesus the law of the Spirit that brings life made me free from the law that brings sin and death.[1]

False guilt involves feelings and beliefs we embrace that often center on pain and rejection. We may believe that God is disappointed with us or that He is withdrawing His love because we continue to have problems and fall short of God's rules of right and wrong. We forget or ignore the clear teaching of Scripture about God's unconditional love and total acceptance and live by our feelings, instead. When life is going well, we think God must be pleased with us. When life is filled with problems, God must be mad at us for something we have done or not done.

Test these statements to see if they are true guilt or false guilt:

⇒ "If you really care about people who are going to hell, you will be here on Thursday night for evangelism outreach."

⇒ "If you're not reading your Bible, you cannot find the authentic will of God for your life."

⇒ "If this church is going to be what God intends it to be, you must give 100 percent commitment to the work of the church."

These kinds of things are what bugged Ryan so much about what he heard from Christians in his family and church. All these statements are designed to trigger an emotional response of shame that will motivate us to change what we are doing to please the person speaking to us. It may work (at least short-term), but it has very bad side effects on the people who receive the guilt. It adds emotional stress they don't need. It doesn't change people's behavior—it just makes them feel guilt and shame. It results in feelings of inferiority, low self-esteem, with-drawal, self-punishment, lying (to cover mistakes), bragging, and aggressive behavior. People who are taught to be motivated by guilt usually learn to motivate themselves the same way—by making themselves feel guilty about how they feel—"If I were a better person, I wouldn't be this way." No wonder Ryan is running away from the false guilt that people have piled on him.

Guilt can go even deeper and become a permanent attitude and outlook in us. We interpret everything that happens or is said to us as a negative message that we did not do enough or that we failed. When this guilt complex gets built inside us, we let all the blame fall on us willingly. We perceive ourselves to be bad people who deserve to be punished.

What false guilt have you believed and absorbed into your life?

What made you believe it was true?

Ryan's criticism of his church is at least partially true. Many guilt-heavy messages can be given out in church. We are told that we are still guilty even after we have trusted Christ to pay for our sins. In churches, where the message of forgiveness and freedom found in Christ should be the central focus, the leaders often use guilt to motivate people to be active and committed to the church.

///

IDENTIFY GUILT MESSAGES
IN YOUR LIFE

What guilt messages did you receive when you were younger, or what messages are you still receiving? See if you can think of one or more and write them down here.

The Message   **The Source**   **How It Influenced You**

Remember Ryan's challenge to Matt? Look at your own Christian life and try to answer his question honestly:

What things in your Christian life do you do just because you want to and because you love God? How much do you do to please others and look good? _____

_____

_____

_____

_____

GUILT SHAPES YOUR
UNDERSTANDING OF GOD

Caitlin, a highschool senior, has been religious all her life. She likes to go to church—the tall ceilings, soft lighting, candles, and organ music make her feel good when she is there. Deep in her soul she knows being in church is right.

Caitlin is very concerned about doing what is right. When she was a child, God had been introduced as an authority figure with lots of power. She remembers being told often, "If you go against God, He will destroy you." So Caitlin does her best to do everything right, but she is afraid that even her best work for the church will not be up to God's standards and expectations. She's not sure what will happen then—will God punish her or delay her reward?

Caitlin's understanding of God makes it hard for her to have a personal relationship with God. Her friends talk about God being their best friend, but she can't understand how that could be true. To Caitlin, God is a disapproving father, unpredictable and ready to punish His children when they do wrong.

All this makes Caitlin feel unworthy of God's love and forgiveness. She hopes it is true, but just in case, she is being as good as she can be so she will get a reward from God when her life is over.

A year ago, Caitlin went through a six-month rebellion and did a lot of things she knew were sinful. During that whole time her awareness of God stayed strong in her mind. During these months of rebellion, she was terrified that God was going to kill her, and that she would die with God mad at her. This tormented her. She had dreams that she was dying and that God was punishing her for disobeying Him.

In what ways does God make you afraid?

Where do we get the idea that God will hurt us if we fail?

Now that Caitlin has returned to church and is living right, she is uneasy and nervous that God truly has forgiven her for what she did. It seems more likely that God will either pay her back for what she did or keep her squirming until the day she dies.

HOW CHURCHES USE GUILT

The message Caitlin gets from the church is that you cannot come as you are with all your problems. She feels judged by the people and leaders of the church for how she dresses and what she does. The focus of her church is on actions and behavior, not on grace and forgiveness. Caitlin is getting the message.

Perhaps this is what makes Ryan so angry. He says that churches talk out of both sides of their mouths. They preach and promise unconditional love and total forgiveness because of the death of Jesus, but they pressure young people to walk in perfect obedience to God and reject them if they don't. It's either act right and perform according to church standards or face the judgment of leaders and others in the church. That's a lot of pressure.

Craig had stopped going to church when he got a job. His Christian lifestyle was slipping, too. He was missing the benefits of being in church weekly and hearing God's Word applied to life situations. When he heard about the death of his old eighth-grade Sunday school teacher, he took a day off work to attend the funeral. When the current youth leader of the church high-school group saw him at the funeral service, his first statement to Craig was, "So this is what it takes to get you back to church?" That had some sting in it.

Apparently the youth leader intended to motivate Craig to get involved with the youth group again. He was counting on guilt and sarcasm to provoke Craig to change his schedule and get to church. It didn't work.

MOTIVATING PEOPLE (WITHOUT GUILT)

Matt thought about his talk with Ryan for several months. It made him examine his motivation for living like a Christian. Was it guilt or something better? It came down to some simple questions: Was his faith just about pleasing himself and/or others, or was his faith truly focused on becoming like Jesus Christ? Here's what he found out:

Be Real. God isn't looking for phonies. He knows what is going on inside us—our thoughts and motives about everything we do. We're not fooling Him. Matt talked to several guys at college who, like Ryan, had junked their faith. They all talked about going through a period of time when they were just going through the motions of being a Christian. One guy was struggling with secret sin; another guy had a tragedy in his family. Everyone needed help, but nobody asked for it. They just covered up their struggle and pretended to be doing fine—same as always. Several months later their faith was dead. Their relationship with Jesus was just a trickle of what it had been. They were too proud to openly talk about what was happening to them—the doubts, the anger, the self-hate, and discouragement. They were like a tree that looks fine from the outside, but termites are eating the inside. When trouble hit them, they snapped and fell hard. Matt felt for Ryan trying to live for Christ with so many expectations put on him by church people who were watching him and his family. It's got to be tough to live in the fishbowl every day. Matt learned being real about your struggles as a Christian is a must to keep your motivation focused on becoming like Jesus and not just responding to the guilt pressure from other people.

> **What sins or struggles do you keep secret from everyone?**

Resist the Lie. Matt learned how right Jesus was when He called Satan the "father of lies." His encounter with Ryan made him reexamine the basis of his faith. He recognized how Satan's big lies about success, seeking the approval of others, and being unworthy of love had influenced his thinking about himself and his relationship with God. Matt committed himself to a regular time of studying the Bible. He's filling his head with God's truth and pushing out Satan's lies. The reminders of God's grace and forgiveness are a daily part of his life. Not only does he feel more encouraged most days, but he is also learning to identify the false guilt when it comes from the church, his parents, friends, and even himself.

Grow from Failure. This has been the biggest change in Matt's life.

Failure previously meant depression and self-pity for Matt. He would say to himself, "I'm just no good." Now Matt is handling failure with openness and a positive attitude. It's become a daily reminder that his relationship with God is not based on his personal success. He understands much better how others feel when they fail and is using his experience to be an encouragement to others. When he falls into trouble, he confesses it to God and asks for help so that he can learn from the whole experience. His sin and guilt no longer condemn or paralyze him. He is free—growing and preparing for what is ahead. Along with his confession, Matt restates the truth that because of Jesus' death on the cross God has forgiven him and made him right in His sight. "I need the reminder a lot more than God does," Matt says.

BREAKING FREE

Matt's faith experience is available to everyone. Sadly, too many follow Ryan's path and live with brokenness and pain. Despite his declaration of being free from guilt, Ryan is finding out that believing Satan's lies brings even more guilt into his life than the misguided, wrongly motivated church people. Satan will make sure that he finds plenty of guilt from new sources and a lot of it from inside himself. Ryan won't find forgiveness and freedom anywhere except from Jesus Christ.

The motivation Matt needs to live for Christ doesn't come

from religious events that are like pep rallies for God. The motivation comes from the heart. "Christ died for all so that those who live would not continue to live for themselves. He died for them and was raised from the dead so that they would live for him."[2] God wants our lives to be loaded with Christ-centered motivation rather than guilt. That motivation comes from inside our hearts, because we understand and appreciate what Jesus did for us. We no longer live for ourselves (worrying about popularity and what others think about us) because our lives have been changed by the living example of humility and self-sacrifice lived out by Jesus. It's not about us. It's about Him.

Remember these steps to break free from guilt and "shoulds":

⇒ Learn to identify the guilt messages and feelings and the results of guilt in your mind.

⇒ Refuse to believe the lies of Satan.

⇒ Focus on the unconditional love and forgiveness of Jesus Christ by reading God's Word and absorbing it into your mind and heart.

⇒ Respond to failure by affirming who you are in Christ as you confess your sins and mistakes.

⇒ Be confident and secure in Christ. Nothing can separate you from His love during this lifelong adventure of renewing your mind and reshaping your life to become like Jesus.

Live guilt-free. Live full of Christ.

///

VERSES TO READ:

1. Romans 8:1-2
2. 2 Corinthians 5:15

8

GET READY FOR CHANGE

"RENEWING MY MIND"

The cell phone was ringing. Brian's hands moved from pocket to pocket, patting each one looking for it. He found it in his jacket on the front seat of his car. He was just dropping off some friends at home after their Bible study.

"Yep," he said as he held the phone to his ear. "You're kidding!" He was almost shouting now. "Yes, yes, yes, yes . . . that's right. It happened this afternoon?" The smile on Brian's face was growing second by second.

"Oh, you bet I remember," Brian said with glee. "I just didn't think it would happen so soon. Where is she now?" Brian asked the caller. "I'm on my way. I'll meet you there in ten minutes. Call her and keep her on the phone so she can't talk to any other guys."

Brian turned his car toward Jackie's house and stepped on the gas. Two weeks ago Jackie, a junior and recent visitor to the youth group, had made a promise at a meeting that she would not date any guys for six months at some point in the future, if and when she ever broke up with her boyfriend. That day was here.

Brian was racing to Jackie's house for good reason. She changed boyfriends pretty fast. Nobody could remember when she had been without a guy for more than a few days, sometimes just a few hours. She had a reputation, and once the word got out that Jackie had broken up with her boyfriend, the phone would start ringing with guys wanting to take her out that weekend.

Hopefully, Diane, who had called Brian, was keeping Jackie's phone busy. Brian was praying, "Please, God, keep her unattached until we get there. Another boyfriend is the last thing she needs. God, help her see that this is her chance to break free from the destructive pattern she has with guys in her life . . . and please don't let me get pulled over for speeding."

We interrupt this story to remind you that you are reading the last chapter of this book. Most likely nobody is racing toward your house as you read these last few pages, but you have the same opportunity Jackie does. This is your chance to break free from whatever negative pattern has been established in your life. Are you ready?

How many times while reading this book did you promise yourself that you would do whatever you could to get out of the negative rut you are in? Probably a voice in your head told you that was a great idea—just not right now. Maybe next month or next year. Don't believe that voice (it's the voice of your enemy). Right now is your time—your chance. In a few pages, you will start *writing* the real last chapter of this book.

TIME TO CHANGE

The time for change in your life is right now. As you grow and mature, your life is filled with changes—some good, some bad. You can handle change. In fact, you should be open to change *now* because the older you get, the harder it is to accept. You know how difficult it is for your parents and grandparents to change the patterns of their lives. This is a prime time in your life to make key decisions that will shape your future.

Change is inevitable. There is no way you are going to be the same person you are three years from now. The big question is, Are you headed toward something better or worse? You get to choose what will influence you during the days and months ahead. What will you feed into your life that will shape the kind of person you want to become?

We all hope for the best, but many days we get down on ourselves and are filled with pessimism when we think about the remote possibility of acting like God. Because we're human, that

How has change been good for you?

In what ways has change been bad for you?

What important changes do you want for your life right now?

seems impossible. But we were given the greatest gift, making anything possible. God sent Jesus Christ into this world to change everything for us. Paul, who experienced a *major* change in his life, reminds us what happens when we put our faith in Jesus Christ. He wrote, "If anyone belongs to Christ, there is a new creation. The old things have gone; everything is made new!"[1] Wherever Paul went and explained the good news of Jesus, people just like us were changed. Putting our faith in Christ begins a lifelong transformation. Not only does God forgive our sins, but He also gives us a new purpose in life, with new attitudes and direction.

Satan, our enemy, stands against change. He plans to tie us down with lies about how unlovable we are and how God could never accept us. His strategy is to deceive us with a feeling of shame (see chapter 5), causing us to lose hope and start believing that we can never change or become what God wants us to be. If we believe his ugly lies, we paralyze ourselves and miss out on what God intends for us to know and do.

MIND RENEWAL

God transforms us into new people *by changing what we think is true.* This book has been an extended compare-and-contrast exercise between what Satan tells us and what God tells us. What we choose to believe makes all the difference. The Bible is very clear—if we believe God, we will experience radical change and become like Christ. Romans 12:2 gives the challenge, "Do not change yourselves to be like the people of this world, but be changed within by a new way of thinking."

This "new way of thinking" goes the full distance for everyone regardless of his or her background. As we read before, Paul explains:

> But what you learned in Christ was not like this. I know that you heard about him, and you are in him, so you were taught the truth that is in Jesus. You were taught to leave your old self—to stop living the evil way you lived before. That old self becomes worse, because people are fooled by the evil things they want to do. But you were taught to be made new in your hearts, to become a new person. That new person is made to be like God—made to be truly good and holy.[2]

God's plan involves teaching us, changing our hearts and minds. He wants to help us remove the old, oppressive lies and replace them with the new, liberating truth.

MIND RENEWAL STRATEGY

God's strategy for renewing our minds has four steps:

1

Identify the Lies.

2

Confess the Lies.

3

Reject the Lies.

4

Replace the Lies with the Truth.

Satan's lies in a person's life are like a virus in a computer. The longer they stay in the person's system, the more damage they do until, finally, the system crashes. You know what a costly mess that is. Let's look at how this works with a real computer.

PROTECTING YOUR COMPUTER

Step 1—Identify

When a virus infects your iMac, the key to saving your system is the knowledge that it is there. When your screen starts flashing or you get weird responses when you try to open files, you know something is wrong. Thank goodness you have installed a virus protection program to protect your machine! Then when the virus hits, your software security force pops a message up on your screen to let you know about the trouble that has entered your computer. Keeping that protection software updated keeps you from getting infected by newly created viruses. Your virus protection tells you exactly what virus is attacking your system and how to respond to it.

Step 2—Confess

When the message hits the screen, you have to respond. You can ignore the warning, or you can believe it and do something about it. Because the virus is not visible to the naked eye, you must believe what the protection program tells you about it. Ignoring the problem won't make it go away. The longer you wait to respond; the more damage will be done to your computer.

Step 3—Reject

A virus brings nothing but trouble. It must be wiped out for the system to survive and to be healthy. The virus is created to damage and destroy. Remove the virus immediately if you want to save your computer.

Step 4—Replace

To make your computer healthy again, you need to remove the corrupted files and replace them with uncorrupted ones. These replacement files must come from an uncorrupted source, be programmed with the correct codes, and be reinstalled properly for the computer to work.

We know how important it is to take care of our computers. Shouldn't we be even more diligent to guard our lives, our minds, and our souls?

Here's how the mind renewal steps work in our lives.

What problems in your life have you tried to ignore, hoping they will go away?

What happened when you ignored them?

GUARDING YOUR SOUL

Step 1—Identify

God's Word is His instruction book, containing the totally reliable list of sin viruses and lies of the enemy that can infect our lives. The more we read God's book, the more alert we will be to the undercover corruption that is trying to infect our lives. As we read and study the Bible, we receive "virus alert" messages—God's Holy Spirit convicting us of sins that are in us and working to destroy us.

Step 2—Confess

As soon as we become aware of a sin, we need to confess it. Confessing means agreeing with God that what we are doing is wrong and destructive. When we are alerted to sin and disobedience, God waits for us to agree with Him and call it what it is. We should not act as though the sin or lies aren't there or that they are not harmful to us and our relationship with God.

Step 3—Reject

God forgives us of that sin and wipes it out. He calls on us to inspect our lives and repent of, or turn away from, any sins and impurities. We reject the lies of Satan in our lives because they are intended to disable and destroy us.

Step 4—Replace

As we remove the corrupted sinful ideas and values from our minds, God desires to fill us with His truth. He wants to replace the damaged parts of our minds with pure and clean thoughts so that our lives operate the way God created us to function.

TIME FOR A NEW LOVE LIFE

When Brian arrived at Jackie's house, she was shocked to see him walking to the door. "What are you doing here?" Jackie asked.

"I came to help you keep a promise," Brian responded. "Anything big happen today?"

"You know? How did you find out? It just happened an hour ago," Jackie said with disbelief.

"Are you ready to keep your promise and commit to going six months without a boyfriend?" Brian said with a twinkle in his eye.

The reality was starting to hit Jackie. Her promise two weeks ago wasn't going to be forgotten.

"I've got a proposal for you," Brian said.

Jackie took the bait and asked what he was talking about. Brian explained his challenge to Jackie. She had been so desperate, moving from guy to guy looking for someone who would really love her. She was the youngest child, growing up late and watching her parents go through the motions of a loveless marriage. There wasn't much love in the house, so Jackie looked for it with the guys at school. Many young men were willing to give her attention and a hands-on physical relationship. But none of them gave her the love she was seeking.

Brian had a different idea. He proposed a six-month relationship with Jesus Christ. He wasn't kidding. He told Jackie that it would mean spending time with Jesus every day, reading about Him and talking to Him about all the private details of her life. "Ask for His kind of love," Brian urged her, "and give Him your love. See if His unconditional love is different from what was offered by the guys you have dated."

The next six months gave Jackie a new look at a life she had only dreamed about. Truthfully, not even her dreams had been this good. Here's how the four steps of mind renewal worked for her.

RENEWING JACKIE'S LIFE

Step 1—Identify

Jackie had huge holes in her life, with unfulfilled desires for love and acceptance from her parents and family. Reading God's Word, she was able to see her situation with new eyes. Her search for love and intimacy became so clear and understandable to her. What became painful, however, was recounting how she had wasted so much of herself with guys who had no love to give her.

Step 2—Confess

This was tearful and tough, but Jackie told the truth about what she was doing when she depended on boys for her identity and comfort. She confessed her mistakes and sin to God and agreed with His Word. She had tried to replace God in her life with human relationships.

Step 3—Reject

The six-month dating ban was a radical life change that forced Jackie to reject the popular version of love and learn how to relate to people without dating them. While the dating was denied, Jackie also uncovered some of the underlying reasons why she was so hungry for love. Not having a guy to cling to gave her the opportunity to build her self-esteem on something other than dating. Her conversations changed. What made her happy changed. How she felt about herself started moving in the right direction.

What radical change would you be willing to make to break a negative pattern in your life?

Step 4—Replace

Jackie was shocked. The thought of not dating for six months had sounded weird. She had thought that praying and reading the Bible would be a weak substitute for the kind of love she usually experienced. But Jesus' love was real. It touched her heart and soul. His love gave her peace in the middle of a home that was breaking apart. His love filled her mind with positive affirmation for who she was, not what she was willing to give. Jesus kept all His promises.

Jackie kept her word and fulfilled the six-month commitment. Her friends made bets about how many hours it would take her to get a "real" boyfriend when the clock struck midnight on the final day. Jackie stunned them by signing up for another six months. And then another six months. Eighteen months plus some more in all. By then she was leaving high school a happier and more fulfilled young woman. She was ready for a boyfriend, but this time what she wanted in a love relationship had completely changed. God had replaced the lies about love with His truth. What a difference!

That was not the end of Jackie's story—it was only the beginning. Since God had become real to Jackie, she opened up her life to His Lordship and let her mind be renewed and changed on a wide variety of life issues and topics: family, self-esteem, struggles with eating and weight, honesty, pride—everything was on the table. The change continues for a lifetime, but she can see God at work in her life. Her imperfections haven't scared God away. She is amazed at how right and good God's ways are for every area of her life.

YOUR STORY

Jackie's story is one of many that you have read in this book. Hopefully they have been helpful to you. But there is one more story that is the most important one—your own story. What's going on with you? What is God doing in your life?

What have you learned about yourself reading these chapters?

Which of Satan's big lies listed below have you battled?

1

Driven by performance to become successful

2

Seeking the approval of others to feel significant

3

Living with blame and condemnation because of your failures

4

Stuck in shame, convinced that you can never change or be different

Following the same mind renewal steps we used to explain repairing the computer and Jackie's life change, describe how you are responding to God's call to freedom in one area of your life.

RENEWING YOUR LIFE

Step 1—Identify the Lies

Step 2—Confess the Lies

Step 3—Reject the Lies

Step 4—Replace the Lies with God's Truth

God never calls anyone to walk on a solo journey. We need each other for support and encouragement. Find someone you trust, and share with that person what you have written (and more) about what God is doing in your life. Encourage each other and grow together.

RECAP

This book was written to help you find the freedom that God offers to you. He has done everything possible to give you a chance to be set free. Finding that freedom means rejecting the lies of this world and replacing them with God's truth. The freedom you seek has been fully paid for and is available to all who put their faith and trust in Jesus Christ. While we will never be completely free until we get to heaven, we can experience much more than we ever dreamed possible if we obey God and build our self-worth on His love for us.

Don't expect perfection immediately. This mind renewal and life transformation is a process and a lifelong journey. Don't worry—God will not give up on us, no matter how long it takes. Don't let pride or fear keep you from giving your life to God. "God is against the proud, but he gives grace to the humble. . . . Don't be too proud in the Lord's presence, and he will make you great."[3] Now get busy. Start writing the last chapter of this book—your story.

VERSES TO READ:

1. 2 Corinthians 5:17
2. Ephesians 4:20–24
3. James 4:6, 10

9

MY
STORY

How God is helping me remove lies and replace them with the truth . . .

TO TALK ABOUT THIS BOOK

OR TO CHECK OUT OTHER

COOL GEAR, VISIT

WWW.THOMASNELSON.COM

TODAY!

Check out these books from Thomas Nelson

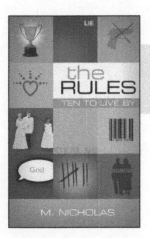

The Rules

How the 10 Commandments are relevant for your life

$10.99 US

Witnessing 101

How to share your faith without freaking out

$10.99 US

Mission: Africa

Take a vacation from everything you take for granted

$11.99 US

The Bible that looks like a magazine!

"Funky, trendy"
– NY Post

"Definitely cool"
– Detroit Free Press

"Anything but boring"
– Washington Times

"A good witnessing tool"
– Susie Shellenberger,
Focus on the Family

THOMAS NELSON
Since 1798

N̄
NCV™
NEW CENTURY VERSION
The Easiest To Understand Translation

In focus groups, online polling, and one-on-one discussion, Transit Books has found that the number one reason teens don't read the Bible is that it is "too big and freaky looking." This fashion-magazine format for the New Testament is the perfect solution to that problem. Teen girls feel comfortable exploring the Scriptures and over 500 further-devotional notes because of the relevant format!